More Adventures of Noddy

Enid Blyton

A SAMUEL FRENCH ACTING EDITION

SAMUEL FRENCH

FOUNDED 1830

SAMUELFRENCH-LONDON.CO.UK
SAMUELFRENCH.COM

FOR AMATEUR PRODUCTION ENQUIRIES

UNITED KINGDOM AND WORLD EXCLUDING NORTH AMERICA
plays@SamuelFrench-London.co.uk
020 7255 4302/01

Each title is subject to availability from Samuel French,

depending upon country of performance.

MORE ADVENTURES OF NODDY

First performed at Wimbledon Theatre on September 27th, 1995, and on tour. The play was presented by James Woods and Justin Savage for Clarion Promotions, with the following cast:

Noddy	Karen Briffett
Big Ears/Kangaroo	Jonathan Broxholme
Bumpy Dog/Monkey/	
The Great Tootle	Martin Wimpress
Mr Plod	David Burrows
Tessie Bear/Tubby Bear	Alexis Beebe
Sly the Goblin/Mr Noah/	
Mr Sparks	Andrew Beynon
Sam Skittle/Lion	Graham Breeze
Sally Skittle/Duck	Sara Jane Derrick

Director	**David Wood**
Associate Director	**Ben Forster**
Sets and costume designer	**Susie Caulcutt**
Incidental music composer/supervisor	**Peter Pontzen**
Choreographer	**Sheila Falconer**
Musical Director/Keyboards	**Cliff Atkinson**
Lighting designer	**Dave Horn**
Sound designer	**Mike Furness**
Noddy's aeroplane UV sequence	**Michael Brydon**

CHARACTERS

(in order of appearance)

Financial considerations limited the number of actors in the original production. Doubling and trebling was therefore employed. Other productions may prefer to use a larger cast.

Big-Ears
Whiskers (a puppet)
Noddy
Bumpy Dog
Tessie Bear
Sam Skittle
Sally Skittle
Mr Plod
Sly the Goblin
Mr Noah
Monkey
Duck
Lion
Kangaroo
Mr Sparks
Tubby Bear
The Great Tootle

Music

Music for the songs by David Wood and the incidental music, composed by Peter Pontzen for the original production, is available from Samuel French Ltd.

Cover Design

The Noddy word mark and Enid Blyton's signature mark are Registered Trade Marks of Enid Blyton Company Ltd - the proprietors and copyright owners of the text and illustrations to all Enid Blyton's NODDY books.

These Registered Trade Marks may not be reproduced for any purpose without reference to Enid Blyton Company Ltd. Samuel French will be pleased to forward enquiries to Enid Blyton Company Ltd.

For further information on Enid Blyton you can also contact http:// www.blyton.com

David Wood would like to thank James Woods and Justin Savage of Clarion Promotions for commissioning this play, and Gillian Baverstock, Enid Blyton's daughter, for her constructive and generous co-operation.

SONGS

NODDY AND THE NOAH'S ARK

1. **The Funky Monkey**   Mr Noah, Noddy,
                              Tessie Bear, Monkey
2. **Mr Noah Had an Ark**   Noddy, Duck, Lion,
       Tessie Bear, Bumpy Dog, Kangaroo, Mr Noah,
                                    Mr Plod

NODDY AND THE TOOTLE

3. **Noddy's Aeroplane**   Noddy and Chorus (sung
                           or recorded as voice-over)

ACT I — **NODDY AND THE NOAH'S ARK**

SCENE 1   Big-Ears' Toadstool House

SCENE 2   The Police Station

SCENE 3   Noddy's House

SCENE 4   The Police Station

SCENE 5   Mr Noah's Ark

SCENE 6   The Dark Wood

SCENE 7   Mr Noah's Ark

ACT II — **NODDY AND THE TOOTLE**

SCENE 1   Mr Sparks' Garage

SCENE 2   A Picnic Spot

SCENE 3   Toy Town Square

SCENE 4   Noddy's House

SCENE 5   Mr Sparks' Garage

SCENE 6   The Sky (UV Sequence)

SCENE 7   Toy Town Square

The two Acts of this play may be performed separately as two one-act plays

INTRODUCTION

In 1993 I was given the opportunity to write and direct *Noddy*, the production which toured Britain for forty weeks, including a London season at the Lyric Theatre, Hammersmith. I was delighted by the response to the play, from parents, teachers, playgroup leaders, theatre critics, and most important of all, the children themselves.

The play combined several stories from the original *Noddy* books, showing how Noddy arrived in Toytown, how he met his friend Big-Ears, who helped him choose his clothes and build a house, and how he acquired his famous red and yellow car. Two naughty goblins caused problems for Noddy, Mr Plod helped solve them. Whiskers, Big-Ears' cat went missing during his birthday party, the animals escaped from Noah's Ark, and a greedy witch tried to get her hands on Noddy's car. Bumpy Dog and Tessie Bear played major roles.

In 1995 Clarion Promotions invited me to write *More Adventures of Noddy*. To find ideas, I re-read the twenty-four original Noddy books, and was given access to a considerable amount of other Noddy material—compendiums of stories, stories in magazines, story strips and other spin-offs of the original series.

I decided to take some of the more theatrical ideas I discovered and to adapt them into two one-act plays, to be divided by the interval. Although most of the ideas and characters were direct from the pen of Enid Blyton, I endeavoured to craft two new stories. I was very pleased when Gillian Baverstock, Enid Blyton's daughter, endorsed the plays, saying that they remained totally faithful to the world of Noddy, as created by her mother.

This world is full of ideas which have appealed to children for nearly half a century. First of all, Noddy may be a wooden doll, but he is really a child in a world of adults (Big-Ears, Mr Plod, Mr Noah, etc.). He is a child learning how the world works, how to cope, how some people are your friends and others cannot be taken at face value; in the books, the themes of fairness/unfairness, generosity, meanness, loyalty and the encouragement of independence are rife; also, as in much of Enid Blyton's work, the theme of justice is very important. I have always believed that children are born with an innate sense of justice. "It's not fair" is a familiar cry from even the youngest children. This also suggests that deep down they know the difference between right and wrong. Although it is always difficult to be dogmatic when discussing moral issues, children do like the rules to be clear and firm. Enid Blyton knew this, and there is never any question as to the actions of the naughty goblins; though not necessarily malicious, they are undoubtedly behaving wrongly and deserve some sort of warning or punishment.

This theme—children learning a basic code of morality—is particularly relevant in the nineties, and it is discussed in great depth by educationalists and child experts. It could well be that, in the last thirty years, our attempts to be more liberal when educating children, and perhaps not dealing with the most basic values, has led to, if not a lack of morality in young people, rather a confusion as to what is acceptable behaviour within a society. The attitudes in Noddy may be simplistic, but I don't believe they are unhealthy. And children never have difficulty in understanding their implications.

Noddy may be a "child" but he has a house of his own, a car of his own and a job (taxi driver) of his own. For children these are the external signs of growing up that they (all too soon!) aspire to. Children love making "dens" or sitting in Wendy houses, driving pedal cars or riding bikes and playing pretend games in which they are doctors, teachers, bus drivers or mothers and fathers; Noddy fulfils all these dreams for real, albeit in a fantasy world

And that fantasy world is, of course, another reason for the success of the books—a world peopled by toys, all of them alive and living in a colourful town; toy engines arriving at the toy station, teddy bears mingling with wobbly men and skittles in the Square; toy cars buying petrol from a toy garage, a Noah's Ark full of real toy animals, bouncy cuddly toys going about their daily business just like people (mainly adult people) in our "real" world.

Another appealing factor of the books is another world, an enchanted magic world of friendly brownies and unfriendly goblins lurking in the Dark Wood. Characters from the realms of traditional fairy tales and the supernatural prove an imaginative source of excitement and fascination for children.

It is my job to take these elements, all of which are truly theatrical, and mould them into the shape of a play (or, in this case, two plays), emotionally involving the young audience, encouraging them to participate, and giving them a very special experience—for many of them their first ever experience of live theatre.

Introduction

In the nineties, it is inevitable and proper that the question of political correctness be addressed when preparing plays for children. I found, when re-reading all the original Noddy books, that the modern editions have been amended to answer some of the criticisms that have in the past been levelled at Noddy.

However, I sense that if Enid Blyton were writing the stories now, she would introduce stronger female characters. This is why I have given Tessie Bear a more dominant role.

Incidentally, in answer to the question several people asked me after the first play, I was unable to use the character of Dinah Doll, from the BBC television series, because of copyright law.

I have to admit that some of Enid Blyton's writing, by today's standards, could be interpreted as rather "twee". I have tried not to be "twee" in the plays, or, indeed, patronising—the most fatal mistake a playwright can make when writing for children.

I am unable to take seriously the criticism of Big-Ears as a name for Noddy's friend and mentor. I cannot really believe that people with large ears are offended by his name. And nobody who reads all the books can honestly say that Big-Ears' relationship with Noddy is anything more than that of a kindly uncle/guardian figure.

I am glad that the mischievous golliwogs have been replaced by equally mischievous goblins. I can see that in today's multi-racial society, the golliwogs could give offence. However, I must admit to being disappointed that the golliwog who ran the Toytown garage has also disappeared. As a child, when I read the early books, this kindly character, who gives Noddy a car, was one of my favourites. Mr Sparks is an acceptable replacement, but I still miss his predecessor!

In her day, Enid Blyton was very much the *Blue Peter* voice of conscience, encouraging children to help worthy causes. For this reason, I have introduced the idea of Tessie Bear organising a collection to help save Noah's Ark.

I have been writing plays for children for over twenty-five years and take it very seriously! I want a play for children to have a proper story, which will involve the young audience and trigger their imaginations. I want them wrapped up in the action, not getting bored and restless. The challenge is to give them a magical theatre experience, the like of which they may not have had before; an experience totally different from seeing something on television or reading a book.

This challenge is in many ways much more difficult than producing a play for adults! Particularly when Noddy, thanks to the current television series, appeals to the youngest of children! But the positive reaction the original production received from thousands of children all over the United Kingdom proved how the magic of Enid Blyton can be translated from page to stage.

David Wood

NOTES ON THE ORIGINAL PRODUCTION

Set

To faithfully follow the spirit of the Beek book illustrations, Susie Caulcutt used a series of one-dimensional flats painted to represent:
1) The Police Station
2) Mr Sparks' Garage
3) Buildings in Toy Town Square
4) A tree

Big-Ears' Toadstool House exterior could have also been made this way, but in fact we used the small revolving truck (exterior and interior) we already had from the first *Noddy* production.

These flats were able to fly into a basic set of cyclorama, cutcloth and three sets of painted legs, depicting a rural Toyland setting inspired by the book illustrations. This basic setting was also used for the Picnic Spot.

Noddy's House was three-dimensional, with enough room for an actor to sit inside, but not much larger! We used the kit version from the first *Noddy* production; this was assembled like a three-dimensional jigsaw on a castered base with curtains for a door.

Mr Noah's Ark was based on a truck with two folding "wings". Two double-hinged doors and a folding-down gangplank provided access.

The UV sequence took place in front of a black cloth. Actors dressed in black carried one-dimensional cut-outs across the stage behind the aeroplane, which was three-dimensional and entered on a castered "trolley". Noddy and Tubby Bear sat inside, then, when the black cloth was in place and the UV lighting on, they *stood*, "wearing" the aeroplane like a hobby horse. The aeroplane had a black skirt to cover the actors' legs. This gave the illusion of flight as the actors slowly walked across the stage.

We considered it important for the scene changes to be effected speedily to keep the action flowing, and the simplicity of the designs helped this.

Props

The most difficult prop is clearly Noddy's car, which really should look as much like the original in the books as possible. We were luckily able to spend a sizeable sum on a "real" car, built on the chassis of a battery-operated golf trolley. But a pedal-car could well have worked.

Whiskers the Cat was a large glove puppet with head and eye movement. The collapsible washing-line post was built into a small castered grassy mound.

For Big-Ears' bicycle we adapted an existing lady's bicycle to look as much like the book illustration as possible.

The Great Tootle's caravan was built along the lines of an old-fashioned bathing-machine, with two wheels, hand rails to pull it, and steps leading down from the double-hinged doors. It was not too large, so that the actor could pull it across the stage in a full circle. When the doors were open for a Great Tootle performance, a bead curtain prevented the audience from seeing inside.

The tootle and Tubby Bear's peashooter need to look very similar. We tried "tin" ones, painted silver, but in the end used wood or bamboo painted white. This helped the tootle to be more visible in the UV sequence.

The UV sequence was created by a specialist. We wanted it to not be too "cartoon-like", basing designs, where possible, on the book illustrations.

Costume

All the characters in the play, except the Great Tootle, are illustrated in the *Noddy* books. Costume designers are advised to consult Enid Blyton Limited, at 40 Shaftesbury Avenue, London W1V 7DD, in order to obtain the correct information for designing appropriate costumes so the characters will look as much like the approved image as possible. But we took the decision not to hide the actors' faces (except for the four Ark animals). Thus Tessie Bear and Tubby Bear wore teddy bear head-dresses with their own faces peeping out from underneath. Bumpy-Dog had a fuller head-dress, but by keeping his head down, the actor created an effective illusion while not having his own face totally masked. The Skittles' head-dresses had holes for the actors' faces to be seen.

The Great Tootle wore an exotic costume, colourfully combining his entertainer image with his roving gypsy life.

Music

Although there are three songs in *More Adventures of Noddy* it is really a play, not a musical. But we used a considerable amount of music, not just to accompany the songs. Incidental music proved invaluable for creating tension and atmosphere and for linking scenes. Underscoring was often used. We used two keyboard synthesizers which gave richness and variety

Notes on the Original Production

to the score. David Wood's music for the songs and Peter Pontzen's incidental music for the original production is available from Samuel French Ltd.

We decided that the tootle music should be played by the musician and mimed by the actor. This gave us more control of the volume, and also meant we could use dramatic licence when Noddy "played" the pea-shooter—it could be the same sound as the real tootle. So a flute/whistle setting on the synthesizer was used.

Lighting
We decided to avoid black-outs whenever possible and let the action flow smoothly from scene to scene. Scenery flying in and out was often in full view or in half light.

Exciting lighting states were used for the magic spells. UV lighting was used for Noddy's flight through the sky.

Sound
Taped sound effects were used not only in obvious ways such as birdsong, owl hoots, the animal cacophony at Mr Noah's Ark, the wasp and the fast forward and fast rewind tape sounds, but also for Whiskers' miaows, Noddy's hat bell and the car's "Parp! Parp!" hooting noises. Special sounds for magic spells and Noddy's aeroplane were shared between the live synthesizer and taped effects. The song, *Noddy's Aeroplane*, was on tape.

Magic
The Great Tootle performed two magic tricks. It may be an idea to employ a magic advisor from the local Magic Circle to suggest and teach two *quick*, visual tricks. We used a specially converted "dove pan"; magic seeds from a large packet were poured into the empty pan, then the lid was placed on, a magic word spoken, the lid removed, and large feather flowers popped out. We also used a "leopard" silk, where spots visibly vanish from and reappear on a silk handkerchief.

OTHER PLAYS AND MUSICALS BY DAVID WOOD

Aladdin
Babe, the Sheep-Pig (based on the book by Dick King-Smith)
The BFG (based on the book by Roald Dahl)
Babes in the Magic Wood
Cinderella
Dick Whittington and Wondercat
Dinosaurs and all that Rubbish (based on the book by Michael Foreman)
Flibberty and the Penguin
The Gingerbread Man
Hijack Over Hygenia
The Ideal Gnome Expedition
Jack and the Giant
Jack the Lad (co-written with Dave and Toni Arthur)
Larry the Lamb in Toytown (co-written with Sheila Ruskin, adapted from
the stories of S.G. Hulme-Beaman)
Meg and Mog Show (from the books by Helen Nicoll and Jan
Piénkowski)
Mother Goose's Golden Christmas
Noddy (based on the stories by Enid Blyton)
Nutcracker Sweet
Old Father Time
The Old Man of Lochnagar (based on the book by HRH The Prince of
Wales)
Old Mother Hubbard
The Owl and the Pussycat went to See... (co-written with Sheila Ruskin)
The Papertown Paperchase
The Pied Piper (co-written with Dave and Toni Arthur)
The Plotters of Cabbage Patch Corner
Robin Hood (co-written with Dave and Toni Arthur)
Rupert and the Green Dragon (based on the Rupert stories and characters
by Mary Tourtel and Alfred Bestall)
Save the Human (based on the story by Tony Husband and David Wood)
The See-Saw Tree
The Selfish Shellfish
There Was An Old Woman...
Tickle (one act)
The Witches (based on the book by Roald Dahl)

Theatre for Children—Guide to Writing, Adapting, Directing and Acting
(written with Janet Grant, published by Faber and Faber)

I dedicate this play to the memory of Enid Blyton, still the children's favourite.

D.W.

ACT I

NODDY AND THE NOAH'S ARK

After a short overture, the CURTAIN *rises to reveal...*

SCENE 1

Outside Big-Ears' Toadstool House, on the edge of the Dark Wood

A washing line is attached to the side, stretching to an upright post. On it are pegged a sheet, pillowcase, a pair of trousers, a scarf and other items

Music as Big-Ears enters from the front door carrying a basket

He begins to take down the washing. Suddenly he sees the audience and reacts surprised

Big-Ears (*gently*) Hallo!
Audience Hallo!
Big-Ears (*putting down the basket and coming forward; louder*) Hallo!
Audience Hallo!
Big-Ears I'm Big-Ears. Welcome to my Toadstool House! You've caught me taking down my washing. (*He returns to work*) It's been a perfect drying morning! (*Suddenly he hears something*)

Whiskers' loud miaow is heard

Did *you* hear something?
Audience Yes.

Another loud miaow

Big-Ears What is it?
Audience A cat.
Big-Ears Yes. He's *my* cat.

Another loud miaow

Guess what I call him? Whiskers! (*He calls*) Whiskers! (*He puts down the basket and searches for Whiskers*) Whiskers, where are you?

Suddenly Whiskers pops up from behind the house

Whiskers Miaow!

Big-Ears can't see him. The audience point, but, as Big-Ears turns, Whiskers disappears

Big-Ears Where is he?

Whiskers pops up again

Whiskers Miaow!

The audience point, but as Big-Ears turns, Whiskers disappears again. This is repeated as appropriate. Eventually...

Big-Ears There you are, you cheeky cat! (*He picks up Whiskers, if necessary going behind his house to collect him*) Come and say hallo!

Whiskers sees the audience and quickly turns his head away

Whiskers Miaow!
Big-Ears Come on. Don't be shy. (*To the audience*) Give him a wave!

The audience waves. Whiskers looks at them

Whiskers (*as if to say "hallo"*) Miaow!
Big-Ears Good cat! Good cat! (*To the audience*) Now today I'd like to tell you a story. All about my little friend, the Toytown taxi-driver called ... anyone know?
Audience Noddy!
Big-Ears I beg your pardon?
Audience Noddy!
Big-Ears Yes! Noddy. One day...

From off stage we hear "parp-parp, parp-parp!" and, with a big musical fanfare, Noddy enters in his car

He stops and sees the audience

Noddy (*nodding, making the bell on his hat ring*) Hallo! (*He gets out of the* *car and waves to the audience. Another nod, another ring*) Hallo! (*He crosses to Big-Ears*) Morning, Big-Ears.

Big-Ears Good morning, Noddy.

Noddy (*stroking Whiskers*) Morning, Whiskers.

Whiskers Miaow!

Big-Ears This is a nice surprise.

Noddy Well, I've just driven Dinah Doll to the station and before driving back to Toytown I thought I'd come and visit you.

Big-Ears Thank you, Noddy. I'm just taking down my washing.

Noddy Can I help?

Big-Ears Yes, please. I'll just give Whiskers some sardines and cream and be straight back.

Big-Ears opens his front door and takes Whiskers inside

Music as Noddy looks at the washing line and the basket. Then he gets down to work. He unpegs a pair of Big-Ears' trousers. Before putting them in the basket he can't resist trying them on. They are enormous on him. He wanders round, having fun, then takes them off and puts them in the basket. Next, Noddy unpegs a sheet. Fun as he attempts to fold it, but "walks up it". He holds it up and can't see, bumping into things and falling over. He decides to lay it on the ground and fold it

Suddenly from off stage we hear animated barking. Noddy looks up in alarm. More barking

Noddy Oh, no! It's... Bumpy Dog!

Music as Bumpy Dog excitedly enters. He scampers all over the sheet, knocks over Noddy and tries to lick him

Big-Ears enters from his front door

Big-Ears What's going on? (*He sees*) Bumpy Dog! Paws off my sheet! Come here!

Bumpy Dog bounces over to Big-Ears, jumps up and knocks him over—into the basket, then tries to lick him

Get off! You horrible hound!

Noddy has recovered and stands up

Noddy Bumpy Dog! Behave!

Bumpy Dog heads for Noddy again. A short chase, during which the washing line post gets knocked over. Noddy ends up on the ground amongst Big-Ears' washing

Big-Ears Oh, no! My washing! It's all grubby and mucky!

Bumpy Dog is barking

Quiet, Bumpy Dog! Go home!

Noddy starts to pull Big-Ears out of the washing basket

Noddy (*suddenly, with a gasp*) Tessie Bear! (*He lets Big-Ears go*)

Big-Ears falls back into the washing basket

Big-Ears Aaaah!
Noddy Where's Tessie Bear?

Bumpy Dog barks

Big-Ears (*struggling out of the washing basket*) She should be here, controlling her pesky pet!
Noddy But she's not! And she wouldn't let him out on his own.

Bumpy Dog barks, urgently, and indicates off stage

Something must have happened to her...

Concerned chord as the atmosphere suddenly changes

(*Deliberately*) Bumpy Dog, where's Tessie?

Bumpy Dog barks and starts to go off stage

Big-Ears He wants you to follow, Noddy. Maybe Tessie's in danger.
Noddy All right, Bumpy Dog. Good dog, I'm coming. (*He makes for the car*) See you later, Big-Ears.
Big-Ears Mind how you go, Noddy. (*He gathers up the washing*) I'd better wash all my washing again.
Noddy (*returning*) Let me take it home and do it for you, Big-Ears. (*He gathers up the remaining items and puts them in the basket*)
Big-Ears Thank you, Noddy. That's very kind of you.

Noddy (*putting the basket in the car*) My pleasure. Lead on, Bumpy Dog.

Bumpy Dog exits

Big-Ears Good luck! Hope you find Tessie safe.
Noddy Bye, Big-Ears.

Noddy "parp-parps" the horn. Bumpy Dog barks off stage

Wait for me, Bumpy Dog!

Big-Ears waves as Noddy drives off

Big-Ears starts to tidy up his washing line

Big-Ears Dear, oh dear! What a morning, eh, Whiskers? (*He suddenly realizes*) Whiskers? Where are you? (*To the audience*) He's so scared of Bumpy Dog, he...

Concerned music as he hurries to the front door and opens it

(*Calling*) Whiskers!

Suddenly Whiskers pops up from behind the house. He is shaking nervously

Whiskers (*nervously*) Miaow.

The audience sees him and lead Big-Ears to him

Big-Ears There you are! (*To the audience*) Thank you! (*He picks up Whiskers and comforts him, or simply looks up at him*) There, there. Calm, calm. You're safe now. (*To the audience*) Hope Tessie's safe too.

A change of gear as he comes forward and begins to narrate

In fact I can tell you that as Bumpy Dog led Noddy back to Toytown, Tessie Bear was making her way to the Police Station...

Music as the scene changes

Big-Ears and Whiskers watch, then exit

Scene 2

The exterior of the Police Station, complete with a police lamp over the door

From off stage, giggles are heard

The Skittles, Sam and Sally, enter, giggling and happily bumping into each other. As they pass the Police Station and start to exit the other side, Tessie Bear enters. She carries a collecting tin

Tessie Bear Hallo, Skittles!

The Skittles giggle and stand in Tessie Bear's way. They shuffle this way and that, not allowing her through

Out of my way, Skittles. I haven't time to play.

The Skittles make disappointed noises and invite Tessie Bear to knock them over

You want me to knock you over?

The Skittles make excited noises

But I've no time! I'm collecting sixpences to Save the Ark.

The Skittles don't understand

Well, you see Mr Noah has so many animals to feed he needs lots of money to buy them food. No money, no food. And no Ark.

Excitedly the Skittles produce a sixpence each. They hold them up

You'd like to help?

The Skittles nod

Thank you. (*She holds out her collecting tin*)

The Skittles indicate, giggling, that they won't put the money in until Tessie Bear knocks them over

You won't give me the sixpences till I knock you over?

The Skittles nod

Oh, all right then! (*She puts down the collecting tin and pushes the Skittles*)

They fall to the floor, giggling with delight. Then they get up. Tessie Bear picks up her collecting tin and holds it out. Sally pops in her sixpence

Thank you, Sally Skittle.

She passes the collecting tin to Sam Skittle, who won't put his sixpence in

Again?

The Skittles nod

Oh, all right then! (*She puts down the collecting tin and pushes the Skittles again*)

They fall to the floor, laughing hysterically

The Police Station door opens and Mr Plod comes out. He carries a rolled-up poster

During the following, the Skittles stand up

Mr Plod What's all this racket? Oh, it's you, Miss Tessie.
Tessie Bear Hallo, Mr Plod. I'm collecting sixpences.
Mr Plod Well, kindly do it with a bit of hush, Miss Tessie. I've important work to do.
Tessie Bear Sorry, Mr Plod.

Sam Skittle puts his sixpence in the collecting tin

Thank you, Sam Skittle.

The Skittles start giggling again

Mr Plod Hey, you Skittles. Scarper.

They hesitate

Sharpish!

Music as the Skittles exit, giggling and bumping into each other

Tessie Bear Will you give sixpence, Mr Plod? (*She rattles the collecting tin*)
Mr Plod What for?
Tessie Bear Noah's Ark. To help feed the animals and do some repairs to
    the roof. We don't want the animals escaping.
Mr Plod We most certainly don't, Miss Tessie. I've got enough to do without
    chasing after missing mongooses or lost leopards.
Tessie Bear Exactly. So will you help? (*She rattles the collecting tin*)
Mr Plod I most certainly will. Come inside, Miss Tessie, and I'll find a
    sixpence.
Tessie Bear Thank you, Mr Plod.

Mr Plod starts to open the door, then stops, remembering the poster

Mr Plod Ah. Miss Tessie, a word of warning.
Tessie Bear Yes?
Mr Plod It's been reported that Sly the Goblin has been spotted.
Tessie Bear Where?
Mr Plod Snooping round Toytown. Up to no good, I'll be bound. (*He hangs
    up the poster on the wall. It reads "WANTED. SLY THE GOBLIN" and
    has a picture of him*) So keep your eye out for him.
Tessie Bear I will.
Mr Plod And keep your other eye on that tempting tin of sixpences...
Tessie Bear (*concerned*) I will.

Mr Plod and Tessie Bear go inside the Police Station

Sinister music as Sly the Goblin enters warily

Sly Hi, I'm Sly. And I mean business. (*He laughs*) Naughty business!
    Let's see, where am I? (*He turns and sees the police station*) Aaaah!
    The police station! Mr Plod's cop shop! Time for Sly to say bye bye!
    (*He suddenly sees the poster*) My, my. What do I spy with my little eye?
    I spy Sly! (*He reads*) "Wanted. Sly the Goblin". What a cheek! I haven't
    done anything yet! But I will now! (*He thinks hard*) Naughty business,
    naughty business. (*He has an idea*) Got it! I'll pinch Plod's poster! That'll
    show him! (*He removes the poster and starts to roll it up*)
Mr Plod (*off*) This way, Miss Tessie.

The Police Station door opens

Sly Aaaah! (*To the audience*) Not a word! Keep your little mouths shut!

He hides behind the Police Station as Mr Plod and Tessie Bear come out

Tessie Bear holds out her collecting tin and Mr Plod puts in his sixpence

Mr Plod There you are, Miss Tessie.
Tessie Bear Thanks, Mr Plod. Bye.

Tessie Bear exits

Mr Plod waves. By this time the audience are hopefully shouting to Mr Plod that Sly has taken the poster. Mr Plod turns to go back inside, then registers that the audience is trying to tell him something

Mr Plod (*to the audience*) What? What's that? (*Eventually he sees that the poster is missing and reacts*) Hey! My poster! It's gone! Who took it?
Audience Sly.
Mr Plod Who?
Audience Sly.
Mr Plod Sly the Goblin? How dare he! Did you see where he went?

The audience point to behind the Police Station. Mr Plod goes to look. Music

Sly emerges round the other end as Mr Plod disappears behind. Sly tries to shush the audience. He crosses in front of the Police Station and disappears behind just as Mr Plod emerges the other side, shaking his head—he can't see Sly. The audience persuade him to look again. After two or three "misses", Sly and Mr Plod both emerge from opposite ends and edge backwards towards each other. They bump and jump

Mr Plod blows his whistle and chases after Sly, who exits. Mr Plod follows. Sly doubles back, but, as he crosses the stage, the Skittles enter and block his path, sidestepping neatly to cover whichever direction he tries to take

Mr Plod enters, blowing his whistle

Sly manages to evade the Skittles, then push them into the approaching Mr Plod. The Skittles and Mr Plod fall over in a huddle. Sly, cackling triumphantly, waves the poster provokingly at Mr Plod

Sly Tee hee hee! Clever old me!

Sly exits

Black-out

As the scene changes, the Light picks up Big-Ears and Whiskers to one side of the stage

Big-Ears Meanwhile, Noddy, led by Bumpy Dog, arrived in Toytown to look for Tessie Bear. He drove straight to his House-for-One...

SCENE 3

Noddy's House

A loud "parp-parp" from off stage. Music as the Lights fade up on Noddy's house. (NB: In the original production, Big-Ears wheeled in Noddy's House, set it, then exited)

Bumpy Dog enters, turns, looks off stage and beckons

Noddy enters in his car

Bumpy Dog barks towards Noddy's House, as if to say, "This is the place"

Noddy (*stopping the car, calling*) Tessie! (*He gets out of the car*) Tessie! (*He has a quick look inside the house, then returns*) Are you sure this is right, Bumpy Dog? She's not here.

Bumpy Dog barks affirmatively

(*Worriedly*) Then where is she?

Suddenly Tessie Bear enters

Tessie Bear (*calling*) Bumpy Dog!

Bumpy Dog bounds over to her, barking with pleasure

(*Making a fuss of Bumpy Dog*) Hallo! Good boy. Good boy. (*She sees Noddy. Rather off-handedly*) Oh, Noddy, there you are.
Noddy (*rather cross*) What do you mean, there you are?
Tessie Bear There you are!
Noddy Where were *you*?
Tessie Bear What do you mean, where were you?
Noddy Where *were* you?
Tessie Bear Coming to see you. Where were *you*?
Noddy Coming to see you.
Tessie Bear Well, here I am!
Noddy And here *I* am!

Tessie Bear That's all right, then.

Noddy (*even crosser*) It's not all right, Tessie! Bumpy Dog came to Big-Ears' house barking his head off...

Tessie Bear I asked him to fetch you.

Noddy (*exploding*) I was worried about you!

Tessie Bear (*realizing*) I didn't think.

Noddy I thought something terrible had happened to you.

Tessie Bear No. I'm sorry, Noddy. Forgive me?

Noddy S'pose so.

Tessie Bear Friends again?

Noddy Friends again.

A brief hug. Bumpy Dog, who has watched the argument with concern, is glad they have made it up

(*Back to normal*) Now, why did you want to see me?

Tessie Bear Well, I've been collecting sixpences. (*She rattles her collecting tin*)

Noddy What for?

Tessie Bear To help Mr Noah feed his animals. I wondered if you'd drive me to Noah's Ark so I can give him the money?

Noddy Of course.

Tessie Bear Thank you, Noddy. I'll give you sixpence.

Noddy No, you won't. I'll give *you* sixpence. For Mr Noah. (*He puts sixpence in the collecting tin*)

Tessie Bear Thank you.

Noddy (*opening the passenger door of the car*) Hop in, Tessie. (*He sees the basket of washing*) Oh, hang on. (*He lifts out the washing basket and heads for the house*)

Tessie Bear What's that?

Noddy Big-Ears' washing. It got a bit dirty, (*meaningfully*) didn't it, Bumpy Dog?

Bumpy Dog gives an apologetic bark

I said I'd wash it again. I'll just leave it inside. (*He takes the washing in the house*)

Tessie Bear puts her collecting tin on the passenger seat of the car, then turns to Bumpy Dog, who barks

Tessie Bear Good boy, Bumpy Dog. Did you find Noddy? You did! You deserve a biscuit. Do you want a biscuit? (*She finds a biscuit in her pocket*

and continues to make a fuss of Bumpy Dog) Good boy. Sit! Sit! Wait for
it! *(Etc)*

Meanwhile, sinister music as, unseen by Tessie Bear, Sly the Goblin enters

*He tiptoes towards the car, reaches in and very deliberately takes the
collecting tin. Hopefully, the audience will shout a warning. Sly tries to shut
them up. Tessie Bear remains unaware of what is happening but Bumpy Dog
suddenly sees Sly and jumps up, barking*

No! No! You don't get a biscuit till you sit! Sit! Bumpy Dog, sit!

Sly exits, triumphantly holding up the collecting tin

Bumpy Dog escapes from Tessie. He looks off stage where Sly exited

Meanwhile, Noddy enters from his house

Noddy Right, off we go. *(He opens the passenger door for Tessie)*

*She starts to get in, then notices with horror that the collecting tin has gone.
Dramatic chord*

Tessie Bear It's gone!
Noddy What?
Tessie Bear My tin of sixpences!

*The audience will hopefully be vociferously trying to tell Noddy and Tessie
Bear what has happened*

Noddy *(coming forward to the audience)* Did someone take it?
Audience Yes.
Noddy Who?
Audience Sly!
Noddy Sly!

*Noddy, Tessie Bear and Bumpy Dog look for Sly but, realizing he has gone,
meet up in a sad huddle. Sad music as they shake their heads*

Tessie Bear *(annoyed with herself)* It's my fault. Mr Plod warned me Sly
    was in Toytown.
Noddy *(hopefully)* Maybe Mr Plod will catch Sly and get the money back.
Tessie Bear *(not convinced)* Maybe. *(She has a sudden thought)* How am
    I going to tell Mr Noah?

Noddy Come on. We'll go to the Ark now. (*He helps Tessie Bear into the car, then goes round to the driver's side. Suddenly he stops*) Bumpy Dog, would you stay here and guard my House-for-One? Just in case Sly comes back?

Bumpy Dog barks

Thank you. Good dog. Keep watch! Be a watchdog!

Music as Noddy climbs in the car and he and Tessie Bear drive off

Bumpy Dog watches them go, then starts to keep watch over Noddy's house. He marches up and down a couple of times, looking important. But after a while he becomes bored. He sits. He yawns. Music echoes his sleepiness. He sinks into slumber. The audience may well try to wake him. In any event, he suddenly wakes up and has a good shake to make himself stay awake. But again he starts nodding off and subsides into sleep. Again the audience may try to wake him. In any event, he suddenly wakes up and, determined to dutifully stay awake, jumps up and struts energetically about. But it is no good. Once again, Bumpy Dog starts yawning and collapses into a deep sleep

Sinister music as Sly the Goblin enters. Attempting to hush the audience he creeps over to Bumpy Dog, checks he is asleep, then carefully enters Noddy's house

In spite of audience reaction, Bumpy Dog stays fast asleep

Sly emerges from Noddy's house carrying Big-Ears' basket of washing

He tiptoes carefully past Bumpy Dog, then checks the coast is clear, then starts to exit. But suddenly he trips and falls. The noise wakes up Bumpy Dog, who, reacting to the audience, spots Sly and—just as Sly is getting up— knocks him down again, into the basket. Bumpy Dog leaps on top of Sly and they "wrestle". Eventually, Sly manages to break free. He grabs the basket and holding it at arms' length, manages to fend off Bumpy Dog, who stalks him. Sly stumbles backwards

Suddenly, Big-Ears, on his bicycle, enters, heading straight for the backfacing Sly

He jams on his brakes, but collides with Sly. Both fall. Bumpy Dog joins in the mêlée

Big-Ears Aaaah!

Sly Aaaah!

They both struggle up

Big-Ears (*realizing*) It's Sly! With my washing! How dare you!
Sly Big-Ears, you clumsy, bumbling brownie! I'll get you!

Music as they start a short chase around Noddy's house and the fallen bicycle. Finally, Big-Ears and Bumpy Dog think they have Sly cornered. They advance. But, in the nick of time, Sly escapes, leaving Big-Ears and Bumpy Dog bumping into each other

Sly exits carrying the washing basket

Big-Ears (*recovering and chasing off after Sly*) Sheet-stealer! Pillowcase-pincher! Knicker-nicker! Come back! (*He stops briefly*) Bumpy Dog, fetch Mr Plod! Quick!

Big-Ears grabs his bicycle and races off

(*Off*) Come back, Sly, come back!

As the scene starts to change, Bumpy Dog barks and urgently circles the stage until he reaches the Police Station

SCENE 4

The Police Station

A folded note is pinned to the door, saying "READ ME"

Bumpy Dog arrives and barks urgently. He bangs on the door with his paw but there is no reply. He expresses frustration. The audience may shout out that there is a note on the door. In any event, Bumpy Dog spots it. But he can't read. He appeals to the audience and points at the words

Audience (*reading*) "Read me".

Bumpy Dog unfolds the note and points to the words inside. He barks a request to the audience to read them

(*Reading*) "Gone to Dark Wood to find Sly".

Bumpy Dog scratches his head. He points to the words again

"Gone to Dark Wood to find Sly".

Bumpy Dog understands. He barks a thank you to the audience and decides to go to the Dark Wood

Bumpy Dog exits

As the scene begins to change, Big-Ears, carrying Whiskers, enters at the side of the stage and continues his narration. (NB: In the original production, Big-Ears, without Whiskers, entered on his bicycle)

Big-Ears So Bumpy Dog chased off to the Dark Wood to find Mr Plod. Meanwhile, I was chasing off after Sly the Goblin. And Noddy and Tessie were driving towards Mr Noah's Ark...

Big-Ears exits

SCENE 5

Mr Noah's Ark

From off stage we hear "parp-parp, parp-parp"

Music as Noddy and Tessie Bear enter in the car and Noddy parks

Tessie Bear Oh, Noddy. What am I going to say to Mr Noah?

Noddy climbs out of the car and opens Tessie's door for her so she can get out of the car

Noddy Don't worry, Tessie. He'll understand. (*He lowers the gangplank to the Ark. He calls*) Mr Noah?

Immediately there is a cacophony of animal noises, making Noddy jump. Animal heads rise up and peep over the deck of the Ark

From the Ark door, Mr Noah enters

Mr Noah (*to the animals*) Calm, shipmates, calm.

The animal noises subside and the heads descend

(*Looking over the deck*) Ahoy there, landlubbers. State thy name and announce thy business.

Noddy It's me, Mr Noah, Noddy. (*He nods, making his bell ring*)

Mr Noah Noddy, welcome! Step aboard!

Noddy I've brought Tessie Bear with me.

Mr Noah (*delighted*) Tessie Bear! (*He hurries down the gangplank to meet her*) Dear Tessie. Kind-hearted Tessie. The saviour of the Ark. Collector extraordinary of shiny sixpences for our worthy cause.

Tessie Bear Well, yes, Mr Noah, I have been collecting sixpences. I…

Mr Noah We won't forget this. (*He looks back at the Ark*) Will we, shipmates?

A cacophony of animal noises. Animal heads rise again over the deck

Tessie Bear Yes, but…

Mr Noah Calm, shipmates, calm!

The cacophony fades

See how grateful they are, Tessie. In this our hour of need you answered our cry for help. The hippos were hungry, the ravens were ravenous and the starfish were starving. But now, thanks to you…

Tessie Bear (*blurting it out*) There are no sixpences.

Mr Noah (*in full flow*) …there are no sixpences. Thank you… (*He realizes*) What? No sixpences?

Tessie Bear No sixpences. I lost them.

Mr Noah Lost them?

Noddy They were stolen, Mr Noah. By Sly the Goblin.

Mr Noah is stunned into silence. A sad, groaning animal cacophony is heard as, disappointed, the animal heads descend

Tessie Bear I'm so sorry.

Mr Noah Alas, dear Tessie, you did your best.

Tessie Bear sobs

Tessie Bear But I so wanted to help.

Mr Noah You did, you did.

Noddy (*suddenly*) We must find another way to help.

Mr Noah Well said, Noddy. No use crying over spilt sixpences. Let's all think hard. How can we raise money to save the Ark?

All think hard

Suddenly, music as Monkey opens the door of the Ark and peeps out. Then he creeps down the gangplank towards Noddy

The audience may shout out that he is escaping, but Mr Noah, Noddy and Tessie Bear are deep in thought. Monkey reaches Noddy and taps him on the shoulder. Noddy jumps and turns as Monkey bobs down and round Noddy and puts his arms round him, lifting him up and spinning him round

Noddy Aaaah!

Mr Noah and Tessie Bear turn to see what is happening

Mr Noah Monkey! Behave!
Noddy Put me down!

Monkey puts Noddy down, then starts tickling him

No! No! Stop tickling. (*He laughs*)
Mr Noah Monkey! Enough!

Monkey stops tickling Noddy

Back on board! We're trying to think.

Monkey sadly starts to go back to the Ark as Mr Noah, Noddy and Tessie Bear adopt thinking positions. Suddenly, Monkey returns, looks cheekily at the audience, without the others seeing, and performs a brief acrobatic trick. He bows, inviting applause. Hopefully, the audience clap. Mr Noah, Noddy and Tessie Bear turn to see Monkey performing another, more impressive acrobatic trick. The audience applaud. Monkey is delighted

Monkey! Stop showing off. We're *thinking*.
Noddy (*having an idea*) Mr Noah, *I'm* thinking I've got an idea!
Mr Noah Launch ahead!
Noddy Well, Monkey's so clever, and I'm sure some of the other animals are too, so why don't we put on a concert, a performance?
Tessie Bear And ask everyone for sixpence to come and watch!
Mr Noah Well, I don't know...
Noddy (*to the audience, hoping to convince Mr Noah*) You'll come, won't you?
Audience Yes!
Mr Noah You will?
Audience Yes!

Mr Noah Very well then! Anchors away and off we go.
Tessie Bear Can I join in?
Mr Noah Of course! (*He indicates the audience*) Everyone can join in. (*Excitedly*) I've just thought. I could sing a song!
Noddy Yes!
Mr Noah I know a song. All about a monkey!

Monkey shows interest

Tessie Bear Sing it now!
Noddy Practice for the concert!
Mr Noah Very well, but (*he takes in the audience*) you must all help.
Tessie Bear How?
Mr Noah By pretending to be monkeys.

Monkey looks offended

Monkey, you just be yourself and show us all how to do it.

Monkey jumps up and down enthusiastically

(*To the audience*) Now, everybody, if you want to join in, stand up!

All encourage the audience to stand

And follow me. And Monkey! Ladies and gentlemen, young ladies, young gentlemen—The Funky Monkey!

Mr Noah encourages everybody to join in the movements, led by him and Monkey

Song 1: The Funky Monkey

Mr Noah

You let your arms hang down
You make a funny face
You bend your knees
And bounce all over the place!

Funky Monkey
Funky Monkey
Funky Monkey
Funky Monkey.

Pretend you're swinging through
The branches of a tree
And you can do
The Funky Monkey with me!

(*Speaking*) Would the grown-ups kindly clap? (*He leads them, clapping in time with the music*)

All   Funky Monkey
Funky Monkey
Funky Monkey
Funky Monkey.

Mr Noah   And then you look around
To find your monkey match
And when you do
You have a jolly good scratch!

All   Funky Monkey
Funky Monkey
Funky Monkey
Funky Monkey.

Funky Monkey
Oh yeah!

All cheer and wave as the Lighting fades to Black-out

SCENE 6

The Dark Wood

In complete contrast to the last scene, the Lights fade up on the shady, mysterious Dark Wood. Music echoes the spooky atmosphere. From off stage the beam of a torch appears through the trees. Spooky sound effects are heard

A shadowy figure enters carrying a torch. As he rounds a tree, we see it is Mr Plod, treading nervously

Mr Plod (*calling tentatively*) Sly! Are you there? Sly!

Suddenly an owl hoots

(*With a jump*) What's that?

Another hoot

(*Talking to himself*) It's all right, Plod. Only an owl. (*He walks on*) Don't like owls. Spooky creatures. Don't like the Dark Wood either. It's eerie in 'ere. (*He starts to shake*) It's creepy and scary and it makes my wees go all knobbly, I mean my knees go all wobbly. Wobble, wobble, wobble, wobble. (*He points his torch on to his wobbly knees*) Oh, pull yourself together, Plod. You're a policeman! And policemen are bold and brave and fearless.

Another owl hoot

Aaaah! This one's not. Not in the Dark Wood, where goblins lurk. Sly! Are you there? Sly! (*He walks on*) I bet there's geasties and bhosties too, I mean beasties and ghosties! Waiting to pounce! Nonsense, Plod. No such things as ghosts! (*He tries to convince himself*) No such thing as ghosts! (*Suddenly he trips and falls*) Aaaah!

The torch goes out

Oh no! I've broken my torch!

Suddenly, from US, *a ghost enters. This white spectre looks behind Mr Plod, then exits the other side. Spooky music echoes its movements*

Mr Plod "feels" something

What was that?

Hopefully the audience will warn him it's a ghost

Again, it enters and hovers up stage

Led by the audience, Mr Plod fearfully looks round. But the ghost moves out of his vision. This happens once, twice, thrice, each time making Mr Plod think the audience is playing a trick on him. (NB: In the original production, there was a gauze insert in the Dark Wood cloth. This enabled the ghost to be lit behind the gauze, which looked very spooky. After three glimpses of it, the audience led Mr Plod to it but, because the light was now off, he could not see it. As he returned, the "ghost" followed close behind him and tapped him on the shoulder.) Finally, the ghost taps Mr Plod on the shoulder. Almost paralysed with fear, he turns and sees the ghost

Aaaah! Help! A ghostie! (*He quivers and quakes and collapses in a heap*)

The ghost throws its white cloak (in fact, Big-Ears' sheet) over Mr Plod, leaving a white pillowcase on his head. We see that the ghost is Bumpy Dog. He bounces up and down, happily barking at the frightened figure of Mr Plod, who struggles out of the sheet. Mr Plod turns and sees the pillowcase-encased head

Aaaah! (*He nervously approaches and pulls off the pillowcase. He realizes*) Bumpy Dog, is that you?

Bumpy Dog barks

Bumpy Dog, that was not funny!

Bumpy Dog gives a laughing bark

I've a good mind to arrest you for impersonating a ghost in order to scare a policeman in the course of his goblin-hunting duties. Anyway, I wasn't really frightened. (*To the audience*) Was I?
Audience Yes!
Mr Plod I knew all the time it was Bumpy Dog, didn't I?
Audience No!
Mr Plod You rotten lot! (*To Bumpy Dog*) Well, now you're here you can help me search for that scoundrel, Sly. He's pinched my poster, he's...

Suddenly Bumpy Dog barks a warning and looks off stage. Mr Plod jumps

Don't do that!

Bumpy Dog barks again

What? (*He looks off stage*) There's someone coming! It's him! It's him! Quick!

He grabs the sheet, and he and Bumpy Dog go US *and hide behind a tree*

Tension music as a shadowy figure slowly enters

Mr Plod and Bumpy Dog suddenly pop out and envelope him in the sheet

(*Triumphantly*) Gotcha!

The captive struggles. Mr Plod manhandles him DS

Sly the Goblin, I arrest you in the name of the law for pinching police property…

The captive struggles

Big-Ears (*for it is he!*) Let me go! Let me go, you silly policeman!
Mr Plod Certainly not!
Big-Ears I'm not Sly!

Mr Plod reacts a moment. Big-Ears throws off the sheet

It's me…
Mr Plod ⎫ (*together*) Big-Ears!
Big-Ears ⎭
Mr Plod I'm sorry, Big-Ears. I thought you were Sly. I'm looking for him.
Big-Ears So am I, Mr Plod.
Mr Plod He stole my poster.
Big-Ears He stole my washing… (*he suddenly notices the sheet he is holding*) my washing! This is my sheet! (*He hands it to Mr Plod*)

Mr Plod studies it. Bumpy Dog barks and indicates the pillowcase on the ground

What? (*He finds it*) This is my pillowcase! Thank you, Bumpy Dog.
Mr Plod Wait a minute!
Big-Ears Wait a minute!
Mr Plod ⎫ (*together*) Bumpy Dog. (*They show him the sheet and the*
Big-Ears ⎭ *pillowcase*) Where did you find it?

Music as Bumpy Dog sniffs along a trail, followed closely by Big-Ears and Mr Plod. Eventually, he disappears behind a tree and barks excitedly. Big-Ears and Mr Plod go to look and bring out Big-Ears' washing basket. They carry it DS

Big-Ears ⎫ (*together*) Well done, Bumpy Dog!
Mr Plod ⎭
Big-Ears (*pulling out his washing*) My washing!
Mr Plod (*pulling out his poster*) My poster!
Big-Ears (*pulling out Tessie Bear's collecting tin*) What's this, Mr Plod?
Mr Plod Looks like a tin.

Big-Ears rattles it

A tin of sixpences.

Big-Ears There's writing on it. (*He reads*) "Save the Ark". Whose is it?
Mr Plod (*remembering*) It's Miss Tessie's. She was collecting sixpences for
Mr Noah's Ark. Sly must have stolen that too.
Big-Ears (*to the audience*) Did he?
Audience Yes!
Big-Ears Thank you.

Suddenly noises are heard from off stage

Sly (*off, chanting*)   Naughty business! Tee hee hee!
                              Naughty business! Clever old me!
Big-Ears Sly!
Mr Plod Quick! Hide! Shh!

*Nearly falling over themselves, Mr Plod, Big-Ears and Bumpy Dog hide
behind another tree*

   Sly enters jauntily

Sly   Naughty business! Tee hee hee!
                              Naughty business! Clever old me! (*He stops down
                                 stage*)
My, my, crafty old Sly! What a lovely, lucky day! (*He counts on his
fingers*) I've got a poster from that fat, pompous policeman...

*Mr Plod, furious, emerges from behind the tree, shaking his fist, Big-Ears
pulls him back*

I've got a basket of washing from stupid old Big-Ears...

*Big-Ears, furious, emerges from behind the tree, shaking his fist. Mr Plod
pulls him back*

And best of all, I've got a tin of sparkly silver sixpences from silly little
Tessie Bear...

*Bumpy Dog, furious, emerges from behind the tree, shaking his paw. Big-
Ears and Mr Plod pull him back*

Mine! All mine! Now, look at the loot! Look at the loot! (*He skips to behind
the tree where he left the loot. After a pause*) Aaaah! Aaaah! It's gone! It's
gone! Someone's nicked it! (*He emerges from behind the tree*) It's not fair!
It's not fair! (*He starts to cry*)

Hopefully the audience laugh at him

(*Seeing the audience*) It's not funny! It's *not funny*! Stop laughing! Shut up! It's not fair! (*He has a sudden thought*) You know who did this, don't you?

Audience No! (*NB: The younger ones may well happily shout "Yes", having not yet acquired the ability to tell untruths in a good cause!*)

Meanwhile, Mr Plod, Big-Ears and Bumpy Dog creep forward, carrying the sheet and pillowcase

Sly You know where my loot is, don't you?
Audience No!

Mr Plod holds the sheet ready while Big-Ears positions the pillowcase on the ground behind Sly

Sly You're a nasty lot of namby-pamby goody-goodies, aren't you?
Audience No!

Suddenly, Bumpy Dog pops round Sly and barks at him

Sly Aaaah!

He steps back, into the pillowcase, which Big-Ears pulls over his legs like a sack in a sack-race

Aaaah!

Mr Plod throws the sheet over Sly's head

Aaaah!
Mr Plod Gotcha! Sly, you're coming to the Police Station.
Sly Aaaah!
Mr Plod Tee hee hee! Clever old me!

Music as Mr Plod leads Sly hopping off back to Toytown. They exit. Bumpy Dog follows, snapping at Sly's heels

Big-Ears retrieves all the stolen goods in the washing basket, watches the others exit, then turns to the audience to take up his narration

Meanwhile, the scene change begins

Big-Ears Mr Noah was so happy when he heard the news! All the sixpences Tessie Bear had collected had been found and the Ark was saved. Now there was no need for the concert. But Noddy and Tessie were so excited by the idea of a special show, Mr Noah agreed to put it on anyway. So now ladies and gentlemen, young ladies and young gentlemen, welcome to Mr Noah's Grand Concert!

SCENE 7

Mr Noah's Ark

A big fanfare sounds. Lights up on Mr Noah's Ark. A banner could proclaim "Welcome to the Show!" or "Save the Ark!"

Noddy enters

Song 2: Mr Noah Had an Ark

This is sung to the tune of Old Macdonald Had a Farm. *Throughout the cumulative song, the audience are encouraged to join in the "Ee i ee i o" sections and the noises*

Noddy (*singing*)   Mr Noah had an Ark
                              Ee i ee i o
                              And on that Ark he had a duck

Duck enters from the Ark

                              Ee i ee i o
                              With a

Duck	Quack quack
Noddy	Here, a
Duck	Quack quack
Noddy	There, here a
Duck	Quack
Noddy	There a
Duck	Quack
Noddy	Ev'rywhere a
Duck	Quack quack
Noddy	Mr Noah had an Ark
All	Ee i ee i o.

Noddy	And on that Ark he had a lion

Lion enters from the Ark

All	Ee i ee i o
Noddy	With a
Lion	R-o-a-r
Noddy	Here, a
Lion	R-o-a-r
Noddy	There, here a
Lion	Roar
Noddy	There a
Lion	Roar
Noddy	Ev'rywhere a
Lion	Roar

All	With a quack quack here
	A quack quack there
	Here a quack, there a quack
	Ev'rywhere a quack quack

Noddy	Mr Noah had an Ark
All	Ee i ee i o.

Noddy	And to that Ark came Tessie Bear

Tessie enters from off stage

All	Ee i ee i o
Noddy	With a
Tessie Bear	G-r-o-w-l
Noddy	Here, a
Tessie Bear	G-r-o-w-l
Noddy	There, here a
Tessie Bear	Growl
Noddy	There a
Tessie Bear	Growl
Noddy	Ev'rywhere a
Tessie Bear	Growl

All	With a r-o-a-r here
	A r-o-a-r there
	Here a roar, there a roar
	Ev'rywhere a roar

> With a quack quack here
> A quack quack there
> Here a quack, there a quack
> Ev'rywhere a quack quack

Noddy   Mr Noah had an Ark
All   Ee i ee i o.

Noddy   And to that Ark came Bumpy Dog

Bumpy Dog enters from off stage

All   Ee i ee i o
Noddy   With a
Bumpy Dog   Woof woof
Noddy   Here, a
Bumpy Dog   Woof woof
Noddy   There, here a
Bumpy Dog   Woof
Noddy   There a
Bumpy Dog   Woof
Noddy   Ev'rywhere a
Bumpy Dog   Woof

All   With a g-r-o-w-l here
> A g-r-o-w-l there
> Here a growl, there a growl
> Ev'rywhere a growl
> With a r-o-a-r here
> A r-o-a-r there
> Here a roar, there a roar
> Ev'rywhere a roar
> With a quack quack here
> A quack quack there
> Here a quack, there a quack
> Ev'rywhere a quack quack

Noddy   Mr Noah had an Ark
All   Ee i ee i o.

Noddy   And on that Ark he had a kangaroo

Kangaroo enters from the Ark

All	Ee i ee i o
Noddy	With a
Kangaroo	B-o-i-n-g
Noddy	Here, a
Kangaroo	B-o-i-n-g
Noddy	There, here a
Kangaroo	Boing
Noddy	There a
Kangaroo	Boing
Noddy	Ev'rywhere a
Kangaroo	Boing

All
With a woof woof here
A woof woof there
Here a woof, there a woof
Ev'rywhere a woof
With a g-r-o-w-l here
A g-r-o-w-l there
Here a growl, there a growl
Ev'rywhere a growl
With a r-o-a-r here
A r-o-a-r there
Here a roar, there a roar
Ev'rywhere a roar
With a quack quack here
A quack quack there
Here a quack, there a quack
Ev'rywhere a quack quack

Noddy	Mr Noah had an Ark
All	Ee i ee i o.

Musical break as Mr Noah enters from the Ark, to applause

Mr Noah	I'm Mr Noah and this is my Ark
All	Ee i ee i o
Mr Noah	And to my Ark one day came Noddy

Noddy takes centre stage

All	Ee i ee i o
Mr Noah	With a
Noddy (*ringing his bell*)	Ting-a-ling
Mr Noah	Here, a

Noddy	Ting-a-ling
Mr Noah	There, here a
Noddy	Ting
Mr Noah	There a
Noddy	Ling
Mr Noah	Ev'rywhere a
Noddy	Ting-a-ling

All

A b-o-i-n-g here
A b-o-i-n-g there
Here a boing, there a boing
Ev'rywhere a boing
With a woof woof here
A woof woof there
Here a woof, there a woof,
Ev'rywhere a woof
With a g-r-o-w-l here
A g-r-o-w-l there
Here a growl, there a growl
Ev'rywhere a growl
With a r-o-a-r here
A r-o-a-r there
Here a roar, there a roar
Ev'rywhere a roar
With a quack quack here
A quack quack there
Here a quack, there a quack
Ev'rywhere a quack quack

Mr Noah	I'm Mr Noah and this is my Ark
All	Ee i ee i o.

Mr Noah	And to that Ark came Mr Plod

Mr Plod enters from off stage

All	Ee i ee i o
Mr Noah	With a
Mr Plod (*blowing his whistle*)	Whistle whistle
All	Here a
Mr Plod	Whistle whistle
All	There, here a
Mr Plod	Whistle
All	There a

Mr Plod	Whistle
All	Ev'rywhere a
Mr Plod	Whistle

All (*gradually speeding up*) With a ting-a-ling here
A ting-a-ling there
Here a ting, there a ling
Ev'rywhere a ting-a-ling
A b-o-i-n-g here
A b-o-i-n-g there
Here a boing, there a boing
Ev'rywhere a boing
With a woof woof here
A woof woof there
Here a woof, there a woof,
Ev'rywhere a woof
With a g-r-o-w-l here
A g-r-o-w-l there
Here a growl, there a growl
Ev'rywhere a growl
With a roar here
A roar there
Here a roar, there a roar
Ev'rywhere a roar
With a quack quack here
A quack quack there
Here a quack, there a quack
Ev'rywhere a quack quack

The music slows down

Mr Noah had an Ark
Ee i ee i o.

Music continues triumphantly as Mr Plod produces, from under his tunic, the collecting tin. He presents it to Tessie Bear. She invites Noddy to join her. Both proudly present the collecting tin to Mr Noah who accepts it graciously. All cheer. Then ... in a big finish...

All   Long live Mr Noah's Ark!
Ee i ee i o!

All wave as—

—*the* CURTAIN *slowly falls*

ACT II

NODDY AND THE TOOTLE

After a short entr'acte, the CURTAIN *rises on...*

SCENE 1

Mr Sparks' Garage

Big-Ears enters, perhaps on his bicycle and parks near the garage. He sees the audience

Big-Ears (*to the audience*) Hallo again!
Audience Hallo!
Big-Ears It's time for me to tell you the story of "Noddy and the Tootle".

Short fanfare

One day, Noddy...

Noddy enters

...arrived at (*he indicates*) Mr Sparks' Garage. (*He stays on stage during the following and watches the action*)

Noddy walks up to the garage

Clanking and banging is heard from the garage

Noddy (*calling*) Mr Sparks! Mr Sparks! Is my car ready, please?
Mr Sparks (*off*) Afternoon, Noddy!

The clanking and banging stops. "Parp-parp" from off stage

Music as the car enters, driven by Mr Sparks

Here you are, Noddy. Good as new!
Noddy Thank you, Mr Sparks.

Mr Sparks climbs out of the car as Noddy "hugs" the bonnet of the car

Hallo, little car. Feeling better?

The car makes a "parp-parp" sound. A Lighting change as the action freezes, apart from Big-Ears narrating. In the following short "flashback" scene, the action is mimed, clearly and deliberately, to Big-Ears' narration

Big-Ears You may be wondering what had gone wrong with Noddy's car. To find out, we need to go back to last week...

Sound effect of winding a tape backwards, as Noddy and Mr Sparks jerkily move backwards

Mr Sparks exits backwards into the garage

Noddy goes round the car and takes from the passenger seat a bucket and sponge. The reverse action and sound stop

Noddy had just started to give his car a wash when along came (*he introduces him*) Master Tubby Bear...

Tubby Bear enters to music. He carries a satchel containing a bottle of lemonade

The mimed action continues

"I do like your car," said Tubby. "So do I," said Noddy. "Can I drive it?" asked Tubby. "Certainly not," replied Noddy. "Please," said Tubby.

Tubby Bear starts to climb in the driver's seat. Noddy pulls him out

"No," said Noddy. "Please," said Tubby. "No," said Noddy. "I don't trust you. You might have a crash. And besides, there's hardly any petrol in the tank." Tubby was a little disappointed.

Tubby Bear exaggeratedly stamps his foot angrily and cocks a snook and pokes his tongue out at Noddy, who starts cleaning the car again

Suddenly he had an idea!

A big gesture from Tubby Bear, accompanied by a musical "ping!"

"Can I *clean* your car?" he asked. "Oh, all right then," replied Noddy...

Noddy hands the bucket and sponge to Tubby Bear, who starts to clean the car

...and went off for a cup of tea.

Noddy exits

Fast music as Tubby Bear, in speeded-up action, cleans half the car, then stops exhausted

Tubby Bear had a refreshing drink...

Tubby Bear takes the bottle from his satchel and drinks

...of fizzy lemonade.

Tubby Bear drinks, then hiccups

Suddenly, he had an idea!

Musical "ping". Exaggerated movement. Then Tubby Bear pours lemonade into the petrol tank. "Glug glug" sound. Carefully, he tiptoes to the driver's door, climbs in, puts down the bottle on the seat beside him, and takes the wheel

In the nick of time...

Noddy enters, sees Tubby Bear in the car, crossly orders him out and chases him off

Tubby Bear just has time to make a rude face at Noddy before exiting, leaving the bottle

Noddy climbs in the car. He turns on the engine. Sound effect of an auto-hiccup! Noddy—and the car—jump. And again. And again. And again

"What's wrong?" Noddy asked Mr Sparks.

Mr Sparks enters and scratches his head

Now back to today...

Sound effects of winding the tape forward. Speedily Mr Sparks and Noddy return to their original positions. Noddy "hugs" the bonnet of the car

Big-Ears exits with his bicycle

Mr Sparks Hiccups, Noddy. (*He goes to a petrol pump and starts filling the car*)
Noddy Hiccups, Mr Sparks?
Mr Sparks Nastiest case of car hiccups I've ever seen. Fizzy lemonade in the petrol tank.
Noddy Oh, no!
Mr Sparks (*replacing the petrol pump*) All clear, now. That'll be three sixpences, please.
Noddy (*dismayed*) Three?
Mr Sparks Tricky job, Noddy.
Noddy (*paying*) Thank you, Mr Sparks.
Mr Sparks (*picking up the bucket and sponge*) Bye, Noddy.

Mr Sparks exits

Noddy Bye. (*He climbs in the car and prepares to set off*)

Tubby Bear enters

Tubby Bear Hallo, Noddy.
Noddy I'm not talking to you, Tubby Bear.
Tubby Bear Why not?
Noddy (*waving the bottle*) You put fizzy lemonade in my car.
Tubby Bear I thought it might be thirsty.
Noddy You thought you'd go for a drive. Well, cars don't run on lemonade.
Tubby Bear Sorry, Noddy.
Noddy You've cost me three sixpences! Now, out of my way, Tubby. I'm meeting Big-Ears for a picnic.
Tubby Bear Can I come?
Noddy Certainly not.

Music as Noddy drives off

Tubby Bear I said sorry!

Tubby Bear shrugs his shoulders and exits

Noddy drives round the stage and the scene changes—the garage flies out

Big-Ears enters, waves to Noddy, then sets out the picnic things (previously set at side of stage)

SCENE 2

A picnic spot

Noddy parks the car and joins Big-Ears, sitting on a rug, enjoying the picnic

As the music ends, we hear birdsong. The Lighting suggests a bright sunny day

Noddy Scrumptious jam tarts, Big-Ears.
Big-Ears (*eyes closed, basking in the sun*) Mmm. Strawberry.
Noddy My favourite.
Big-Ears What a perfect afternoon.

Suddenly the angry buzzing of a wasp is heard. Big-Ears takes no notice, but Noddy reacts nervously

Noddy What's that?
Big-Ears What's what?
Noddy That "bzz bzz" noise.
Big-Ears A fly.
Noddy (*jumping up*) It's not! It's a wasp! (*He leaps around*) I hate wasps! Go away! Buzz off somewhere else!
Big-Ears (*still calm*) Take no notice of it, Noddy. It's not interested in you.
Noddy It's *very* interested in me! Buzz off! Aaah!
Big-Ears It won't sting you if you stay still. (*He gets up and bends down to look in the picnic basket*)
Noddy I'd rather not take the risk.

The buzzing stops. Then starts. Then stops

Where are you? Where are you? (*He suddenly sees the wasp on Big-Ears' bottom and takes off his shoe*) Aha! Stay still, Big-Ears.
Big-Ears Exactly. Stay still and it won't sting you.

Noddy whacks Big-Ears on the bottom with his shoe

(*Leaping up*) Aaaah! I've been stung! I've been stung!

The buzzing starts again

Noddy No, you haven't.
Big-Ears (*seeing the shoe and realizing what has happened*) Noddy, how could you? (*He rubs his bottom*)

The buzzing fades away

Noddy Sorry, Big-Ears. It's gone, anyway. Have another jam tart.
Big-Ears (*rather grudgingly*) Mmm.

Both sit again. Noddy puts his shoe back on. Big-Ears eats a jam tart. Suddenly Noddy looks up and sees something

Noddy Look, Big-Ears!

Music as a family of birds flies overhead, travelling slowly from one side of the stage to the other, then exiting. (In the original production this proved impractical; the birds' flight was imagined)

I wish I would fly, like a bird. Swooping and soaring, diving and gliding, high in the sky.
Big-Ears You'd need to grow a pair of wings, Noddy.
Noddy I've got a pair of arms! (*He flaps his arms and stretches up. But he can't fly. He climbs on the driving seat of the car, flaps his arms and jumps. He falls to the ground*) Ow!
Big-Ears (*laughing*) I'm afraid flying's not for you, little friend.
Noddy (*standing up*) Ow! (*He rubs his leg*)
Big-Ears What is it now?
Noddy Ow! (*He rubs his arm*) I've been stung, Big-Ears. It's that wretched wasp again. Ow! (*He rubs his other leg*)
Big-Ears (*coming to investigate*) I can't hear a wasp. (*He bends over to look at Noddy's leg*) Ow! (*He rubs his bottom*)

Tubby Bear enters with a peashooter. He takes aim and blows

Ow! (*He rubs his arm*)

Tubby Bear aims again. He blows

Noddy Ow! (*He rubs his other arm. Suddenly he spots Tubby Bear*)

Tubby Bear laughs

It's Tubby!
Big-Ears (*to Tubby Bear*) What are you doing?
Tubby Bear Playing with my peashooter! (*He takes aim and blows again*)
Big-Ears Ow! Stop it!
Noddy Buzz off, Tubby! You're more nuisance than a wasp. Buzz off!

Tubby Bear laughs, pulls a face and runs off

Big-Ears Cheeky little bear!

Music

(*To the audience*) It was time for Noddy to go back to work...

Noddy climbs in his car and drives off

Big-Ears waves and clears up the picnic things

...and for me to go home to my Toadstool House. We agreed to meet next day in Toytown Square.

Big-Ears exits as the scene changes

SCENE 3

Toytown Square

Music

The Skittles enter, giggling and bumping into each other

As they cross the Square they notice something off stage coming towards them. They back away, curious but somewhat nervous

The Great Tootle enters, an itinerant entertainer. He pulls behind him a small caravan, rather like an old-fashioned bathing-machine. A painted sign along the top proclaims his name

He parks the caravan in a good spot. Then he unloads a drum or a tambourine and begins to bang it

The Great Tootle (*speaking in rhyme and rhythm*)
          Roll up! Roll up! Don't be shy!
          It's your lucky day! Let me tell you why!
          Roll up! Roll up! Don't be late!
          Show time! Show time! It's gonna be great!

He bangs his drum or shakes his tambourine as, from opposite sides,

Tubby Bear and Noddy enter, drawn by the noise. They join the Skittles to form an audience

> Citizens of Toytown, good day!
> Gather round! Hear what I say!
> I'm the Great Tootle and I want you to know
> Tomorrow you can see my magic show!
> Tell your friends to come on down!
> Tomorrow the Tootle is coming to town!
> Wonders, miracles, spells and tricks!
> See the Great Tootle, tomorrow at six! (*He starts to
> put his drum away*)

His audience is disappointed

Noddy Can't we see some magic *now*?
Tubby Bear Yes, please!

The Skittles squeal excitedly

The Great Tootle Sorry, my friends. Come back tomorrow.
Noddy Now! Now! Now!
Tubby Bear Now! Now!
The Great Tootle (*quietening them*) All right! All right! Watch and wonder!
(*He performs an impressive magical trick*) Iggery, jiggery, toot toot toot!
Da daaaa!

Noddy, Tubby Bear and the Skittles applaud and cheer

Noddy⎫ (*together*) More! More!
Tubby Bear⎭
The Great Tootle All right! (*He shows them a musical instrument that looks
like a penny whistle; it also resembles Tubby Bear's peashooter*) This, my
friends, is very special. Truly magical.
Noddy What is it?
The Great Tootle A tootle.
Tubby Bear A tootle?
The Great Tootle A tootle.
Noddy What does it do?
The Great Tootle It tootles.
Tubby Bear Tootles?
The Great Tootle Tootles. And when the tootle tootles, its mysterious magic
powers make people happy, so happy!

Noddy How?
The Great Tootle The Great Tootle will show you. (*Dramatically he raises the tootle to his lips and starts to play a jolly tune like an Irish jig*)

Suddenly, as the power of the tootle's music takes them over, Noddy, Tubby Bear and the Skittles start to dance. First their feet tap, then their legs kick out until they are jumping and jigging with abandon

Tubby Bear What's happening?
Noddy We're dancing. We can't help it!

The Skittles whoop with delight

Mr Sparks enters

He heads across the square looking serious. But he suddenly stops and listens to the music. A joyous smile spreads across his face and he starts to dance

Mr Sparks What's going on? I feel so happy!
Noddy It's the Great Tootle's tootle, Mr Sparks. It's magic!

All continue dancing

Big-Ears enters

Big-Ears (*waving*) Hallo, Noddy. (*He crosses to the dancing Noddy*)
Noddy Big-Ears! Hallo!
Big-Ears Noddy, why are you … oh! (*He starts to dance uncontrollably*) Oooh! Ah! Wheee! Ha! Ha!

Everybody laughs and cheers. The general dancing continues and gets wilder

Mr Plod enters, blowing his whistle

Mr Plod Stop! In the name of the law!

The Great Tootle stops playing. Groans of disappointment as everyone begins to stop dancing

What's all this noise and abandoned activity?
Noddy We're dancing, Mr Plod.
Big-Ears To the tootle. It's wonderful!

Mr Sparks We're all very happy, Mr Plod.
Tubby Bear Thanks to the tootle!
Mr Plod Tootle? What tootle?
The Great Tootle This tootle! (*He starts to play again*)

Everyone starts happily dancing again

Mr Plod Stop it! Stop it! Dancing's not allowed in the Square ... oh!
(*Suddenly the magic of the tootle affects him and he starts dancing*) Ah!
Ooh! Wheee! Ha, ha, ha.

The others cheer and egg him on. After a while...

No! No! No! (*He manages to blow his whistle*) Stop! Stop it. (*He pushes
through to the Great Tootle*) Stop this er ... tootling at once!

*The Great Tootle stops playing. All stop dancing. Groans of disappointment.
Mr Plod brings the Great Tootle down stage*

You can't cause a crowd like this, you know. Not in the Square. (*He takes
out his notebook*) Name?
The Great Tootle The Great Tootle. (*He produces a piece of paper*) I have
permission to perform here.
Mr Plod (*looking at the piece of paper*) Not till tomorrow, you haven't. (*To
the others*) Now, move along there, move along.

Everyone starts to reluctantly move off

(*To the Great Tootle*) What sort of music do you call that, anyway?
The Great Tootle I call it foot-music. Your feet hear it and dance. (*He plays
one note*)

Mr Plod involuntarily lifts a leg, then controls it

Mr Plod Huh. Most undignified if you ask me. (*He turns away and ushers
the others away*) Now, then. Move along. Foot-music, indeed.

All exit, except the Great Tootle who returns to his caravan

Noddy comes back and approaches the Great Tootle

Noddy Great Tootle, I really enjoyed that.
The Great Tootle Good! And you are...?

Noddy I'm Noddy. (*He nods his head and rings his bell*)
The Great Tootle Delighted to meet you, Noddy. I like your bell.
Noddy I like your tootle. Could I play it? I'd love to make people dance.
The Great Tootle Sorry, Noddy. Only the Great Tootle tootles!
Noddy (*sadly*) I see. (*He turns to go*)
The Great Tootle Noddy, wait!

*Noddy turns. Magical music starts as the Great Tootle beckons Noddy back
and takes out a three-coloured magic wand*

(*Chanting like a spell*)   This wishing wand is just for you
                            Three wishes you can make come true.
                            It's magic, Noddy, wait and see...
                            But use your wishes carefully! (*He hands Noddy the
                            wand*)
Noddy (*thrilled*) I will! Thank you, Great Tootle.
The Great Tootle See you at my show tomorrow?
Noddy Of course.

Noddy exits in a daze

The Great Tootle returns to his caravan and goes inside

Music suggests the passage of time as the Lights fade to moonlight

*Then, through the shadows, someone enters surreptitiously and crosses to
the caravan. It is, in fact, Tubby Bear, but the audience should not be
absolutely aware of who it is. He enters the caravan and, after a few
seconds, emerges. Has he stolen something? He scampers off into the
shadows as the Lighting fades to Black-out*

SCENE 4

Noddy's House

Next morning

*Lights up as Noddy emerges from his house, excitedly carrying the wishing
wand he was given. He talks to himself, sharing his thoughts with the
audience, not talking directly to them*

Noddy (*looking at the wand*) Three wishes! I can't believe it! "Use them

carefully," he said. I will, Great Tootle! Don't want to waste them! Now,
let's think. What do I want to wish for? I already have a nice house. And
a splendid car. And a job I love, driving it. I'm really very lucky. So what
shall I wish for? Oh, I wish I could think of a really good wish…

Flash. Dramatic Lighting and sound effects

(*Reacting*) What's going on? (*He realizes*) Oh no, I made a wish! I've
wasted one! I wished I could think of a wish! How stupid!

A musical "ping" as Noddy thinks of something

(*With a gasp*) It's worked! I've *thought* of something to wish for! To fly
in the sky! Like those birds Big-Ears and I saw at the picnic! Yes! Right.
Here goes. (*He stands in a wishing position and concentrates*) I wish…

Suddenly Tubby Bear enters cheekily and blows his peashooter at Noddy

Ow! (*He rubs his arm and turns*) Tubby Bear. Not again. Go away! (*He
hides his wand*)
Tubby Bear What are you doing, Noddy?
Noddy Nothing.
Tubby Bear Can I join in?
Noddy No.
Tubby Bear I'm bored.
Noddy You're boring.
Tubby Bear Please.
Noddy No.

Tubby Bear raises his peashooter

And put that peashooter away!
Tubby Bear Shan't!

But, as Noddy advances, he puts it in his pocket

You wouldn't let me come to your picnic!
Noddy You put fizzy lemonade in my car!
Tubby Bear Can't catch me!

*As Noddy tries to grab him, Tubby Bear escapes, then takes out the tootle and
plays it. Noddy stops in his tracks. He starts to dance*

Noddy What's going on? Help! (*He realizes*) It's the tootle! Tubby, you've
got the tootle!

Tubby nods, but goes on playing. Noddy carries on dancing

How did you get it? Did you steal it? Did you, Tubby? (*To the audience*) Did he steal it?

Audience Yes!

Noddy (*dancing towards Tubby Bear*) How could you, Tubby? The Great Tootle needs it for his show. Give it here. (*He makes an unsuccessful grab for it*)

Tubby Bear stops playing and runs away

Give it to me and I'll give it back to the Great Tootle.

Tubby Bear (*putting the tootle in his pocket*) Shan't.

Noddy You bad bear. Give it here!

Tubby thinks

Tubby Bear (*rather shamefaced*) Oh all right, then. (*He takes the tootle out of his pocket and hands it over*)

Noddy quickly pockets it

Noddy (*meaningfully*) Bye, Tubby.

Tubby reluctantly turns and stomps off

Right. (*He produces his wand*) Here goes! (*He takes up his wishing position*) I wish...

Suddenly Tubby Bear enters—playing the tootle again

Noddy starts to dance

Oh no, not again! Tubby, how did you...? (*Still dancing, he looks in his pocket and takes out...*) ...The peashooter! You didn't give me the tootle, you gave me your pesky peashooter!

Tubby Bear nods gleefully and carries on playing. Noddy, dancing, advances on him

Tubby, I'm fed up with you! I wish you'd buzz off! Buzz off up to the clouds and don't come back!

Flash. Magical Lighting and sound effects. Tubby Bear immediately stops playing, stiffens and starts to buzz

(Realizing what he has done) Oh no! I didn't mean it!

But it's too late. Tubby Bear starts to "buzz off". He flaps his arms, nearly runs into Noddy, who has to sidestep, then does a long run, buzzing loudly, and vanishes off stage

Exciting take-off noises. Noddy watches off stage as Tubby Bear achieves lift-off, then follows his flight over the heads of the audience. (Optional) Suddenly, a puppet Tubby Bear flies over Noddy's head, up and away. The sound effects fade

(Beginning to panic) What have I done? I've wasted my second wish and Tubby's taken off! Help! What am I going to do? *(He has a sudden idea)* Big-Ears! If only I had Big-Ears here, he'd know what to do. *(Dramatically, still holding the wand)* I wish I had Big-Ears...!

Big Flash. Lighting and sound effects. Noddy retreats behind his house. As the smoke clears and the effects die down...

(From behind the house, calling softly) Big-Ears. Are you here? *(He creeps round the house. We see that he has acquired enormous ears. But he doesn't realize yet)* Big-Ears? Big-Ears!

The audience will probably shout out to Noddy about his big ears. In any event, he suddenly becomes aware of them

(Almost silent with shock) Aaaah! I didn't! I couldn't have! I did! I wished for Big-Ears and I've *got* big ears ... and it was my last wish! *(Suddenly he hears a voice from off stage)*
Mr Plod *(off)* This way, sir. We'll soon sort this out.

Noddy reacts with horror, thinks, then dives into his house

Mr Plod and the Great Tootle enter. The Great Tootle is very angry. Mr Plod leads the way to Noddy's house

Noddy, it's Mr Plod. Are you in there?
Noddy *(off, after a slight pause)* Er ... yes, Mr Plod.
Mr Plod Could you kindly step outside?
Noddy Er ... no, Mr Plod.
Mr Plod No?
Noddy I can't!
Mr Plod You can't? *(To the Great Tootle)* He can't.

The Great Tootle He must!
Mr Plod (*to Noddy*) You must!
Noddy I won't!
Mr Plod (*to the Great Tootle*) He won't!
The Great Tootle He will!
Mr Plod He won't!

Big-Ears enters

The Great Tootle He will!
Mr Plod He won't!
Big-Ears What's going on?
Mr Plod Big-Ears! Noddy says he won't come out. (*He watches the following exchange like a tennis match*)
Big-Ears Why not?
The Great Tootle He's afraid to face *me*, that's why.
Big-Ears (*recognizing him*) Good day, Great Tootle.
The Great Tootle What's good about it? I've lost my tootle.
Big-Ears I beg your pardon?
The Great Tootle My tootle! It disappeared during the night. This ... Noddy showed great interest in my tootle. (*Accusingly*) I think he knows where it is!
Big-Ears (*vehemently*) Noddy would never steal, Great Tootle.
The Great Tootle Prove it!
Mr Plod (*intervening*) Big-Ears. You're Noddy's friend. Maybe you could talk to him. Find out what's what.
The Great Tootle Find my tootle, more like.
Big-Ears I will. Come back in five minutes, Mr Plod.
Mr Plod Thank you, Big-Ears. Come along, sir. Five minutes.

Mr Plod escorts a reluctant Great Tootle. They exit

Big-Ears (*calling into the house*) Noddy? It's me, Big-Ears.
Noddy Have they gone?
Big-Ears Yes. Come on out.
Noddy Promise you won't laugh?
Big-Ears Of course not. Why?

Noddy comes out, highly embarrassed. He still holds the wand

Big-Ears sees his huge ears and burst out laughing

Noddy You said you wouldn't laugh!

Big-Ears (*trying to stop laughing*) I'm sorry, my friend, but... (*he points to himself*) Big-Ears, (*he points to Noddy*) Bigger-Ears! (*He laughs, then manages to control himself*) I'm sorry. What happened?

Noddy (*blurting forth*) The Great Tootle gave me a wishing wand and it all went wrong and Tubby Bear took off and I wanted you to be here so I said "I wish I had Big-Ears", and now I've got big ears and they're horrible and I haven't any wishes left so I'm stuck with them forever! (*He dissolves into tears*)

Big-Ears puts his arm round Noddy and takes away the magic wand

Big-Ears I see. It can be very dangerous meddling with magic, Noddy.
Noddy What am I going to do?
Big-Ears Well, for a start, stop crying. Now listen, we'll try to *reverse* the wishing spell. That's quite different from making a *new* wish.
Noddy Really?
Big-Ears Really. Now, where were you standing when you made the wish?
Noddy (*finding the place*) Here.
Big-Ears And what exactly did you say?
Noddy I said "I wish I had Big-Ears".
Big-Ears Right. You must say it backwards! (*He gives Noddy back the magic wand*)
Noddy Backwards?
Big-Ears To reverse the spell. (*He concentrates*) Ears Big had I wish I! Ready? I'll help. (*To the audience*) We'll all help, won't we?
Audience Yes!
Big-Ears Say after me...

Noddy concentrates, in his wishing position. Atmospheric music and lighting

Ears!
Noddy and Audience Ears!
Big-Ears Big!
Noddy and Audience Big!
Big-Ears Had!
Noddy and Audience Had!
Big-Ears I!
Noddy and Audience I!
Big-Ears Wish!
Noddy and Audience Wish!
Big-Ears I!
Noddy and Audience I!

Music, Lighting and sound effects as Noddy backs to behind the house. Big flash. Noddy steps through the smoke. The big ears have gone

Big-Ears We did it!

Cheers as Noddy thankfully feels his own ears

Noddy Thank you, Big-Ears. (*To the audience*) Thank you everybody.
Big-Ears Now, Noddy, what's all this about the tootle?
Noddy (*deflated*) Oh, no! The tootle.
Big-Ears The Great Tootle thinks you took it.
Noddy I didn't, Big-Ears. Tubby Bear took it.
Big-Ears Tubby, I might have guessed. Well, we must find him at once and get it back.
Noddy We can't. (*Rather shamefaced*) Tubby's taken off.
Big-Ears Taken off?
Noddy Oh, Big-Ears. (*He blurts forth*) I didn't mean to, really, but he started blowing his peashooter again and being a real nuisance and I had the wishing wand in my hand and...
Big-Ears You didn't wish he'd go away?
Noddy (*nodding*) "Up to the clouds and don't come back".
Big-Ears And he...
Noddy Took off! With the tootle!
Big-Ears Noddy, how could you? (*He can't help smiling*) I wish I'd seen it.
Noddy (*having an idea*) Big-Ears. We couldn't reverse *that* wishing spell too, could we? Get Tubby back. Please.
Big-Ears I think we should try.

Noddy stands ready

Now what exactly did you say?
Noddy I said, "Tubby, I wish you'd buzz off. Up to the clouds and don't come back!"
Big-Ears Mmm. (*He concentrates*) Back come don't and. Clouds the to up. Off buzz you'd. Wish I Tubby. (*To Noddy*) Say it after me. (*To the audience*) Everybody! (*He strikes a magical pose*)

Magical Lighting and music

(*Chanting*) Back come don't and!
Noddy and Audience Back come don't and!
Big-Ears Clouds the to up!
Noddy and Audience Clouds the to up!
Big-Ears Off buzz you'd!
Noddy and Audience Buzz off you'd!
Big-Ears Wish I Tubby!
Noddy and Audience Wish I Tubby!

Music, Lighting and sound effects. (Optional) The puppet Tubby Bear flies backwards overhead, descending off stage. Noddy and Big-Ears see his descent, following it off stage

Buzzing noise as Tubby Bear enters in reverse back to where he started his take-off

Music, Lighting and sound effects end. Tubby Bear "wakes up"

Big-Ears Well done, everybody!
Tubby Bear Cor, Noddy. How did you do that?
Noddy (*showing him*) The wishing wand did it. Sorry, Tubby.
Tubby Bear That's all right. I enjoyed it. Mind you, that cloud was freezing.
Big-Ears Right! I'll fetch Mr Plod and the Great Tootle.

Big-Ears exits

Tubby Bear (*nervously*) What for?
Noddy So you can say sorry and give back the tootle.
Tubby Bear The tootle! (*He searches for it*) Noddy, it's gone!
Noddy But you had it!
Tubby Bear I must have left it on the cloud.
Noddy Oh no! (*He looks off*) They're coming! What are we going to do?
Tubby Bear Mr Plod might put me in prison!
Noddy We'll just have to tell them.
Tubby Bear No! (*He has an idea*) Where's my peashooter?
Noddy (*producing it from his pocket*) Here.
Tubby Bear It looks like the tootle. Couldn't we give him that?
Noddy Of course not ... unless...
Tubby Bear What?
Noddy (*thinking aloud*) Well, if I played the peashooter like the tootle, and if you... (*he notices the audience*) if *everyone* pretended it made them dance...
Tubby Bear The Great Tootle might think it was the *real* tootle!
Noddy (*to the audience*) Will you help? Otherwise we'll be in big trouble. Please will you help?
Audience (*hopefully*) Yes!
Noddy Let's have a practice. Come on, everybody, get up and dance! (*He "blows" the peashooter, imitating the jig tune*)

Tubby Bear leads the audience dancing. After a while, he looks off stage

Tubby Bear They're coming!

Noddy Right. Sit down, everyone. But, please, when I play, you dance! (*He settles the audience, then hands the peashooter to Tubby Bear*)

Tubby Bear hides behind Noddy

Big-Ears, Mr Plod, and the Great Tootle enter

Mr Plod Ah, Noddy. Are you feeling quite yourself again?
Noddy Yes, thank you, Mr Plod.
The Great Tootle Where's my tootle?
Noddy (*stepping aside to reveal Tubby Bear*) Great Tootle, Tubby Bear has something to say.
Tubby Bear (*with difficulty*) Mr Great Tootle, I took your tootle and I'm very sorry. Here it is. (*He holds up the peashooter*)
The Great Tootle (*delighted*) My tootle!
Mr Plod Tubby, you're a naughty bear. I've a good mind to put you in prison.
The Great Tootle No, no, Mr Plod. No need for that. As long as I have my tootle back.

Mr Plod collects the peashooter from Tubby Bear and begins to take it to the Great Tootle who reaches for it

Mr Plod Very well, sir. Think yourself lucky, Tubby.
Noddy (*stepping between Mr Plod and the Great Tootle*) Great Tootle, please could I play your tootle. Just once?
The Great Tootle Well...
Big-Ears Seems fair enough to me. Eh, Mr Plod?
Mr Plod (*to the Great Tootle*) Well, seeing as how you thought Noddy had taken it when he hadn't...
The Great Tootle Very well. Noddy, I'm sorry I suspected you. Of course you can play my tootle.
Noddy Thank you. (*He takes the peashooter from Mr Plod*) I'd love to make everyone dance!
Mr Plod Eh? I don't want to dance. Dancing makes a policeman look silly.
Big-Ears Put your fingers in your ears.
Mr Plod What?
Big-Ears Then you won't hear the music.
Mr Plod (*understanding*) So I won't! So I will! (*He puts his fingers in his ears*)
Noddy (*meaningfully*) Ready, everyone? (*He "plays" the peashooter*)

The audience dances. Tubby Bear dances, then sees that Big-Ears isn't dancing

Tubby Bear (*going to Big-Ears*) Come on, Big-Ears, dance!
Big-Ears What? Oh! Yes! (*Bemused, he starts dancing*)

After a while, Noddy stops "playing". Everyone cheers

Noddy (*quickly placing the peashooter in the Great Tootle's pocket*) Thank
   you, Great Tootle.
The Great Tootle Thank *you*, Noddy. See you at my show!

*All say goodbye as the Great Tootle starts to exit. All, that is, except Mr Plod,
who still has his fingers in his ears. The Great Tootle removes Mr Plod's
fingers from his ears and takes him off*

Mr Plod Oh! Thank you, sir. Bye everybody.

   Mr Plod and the Great Tootle exit

Noddy (*to the audience*) Thank you!
Big-Ears (*bemused*) Noddy, it's funny how today my feet didn't want to
   dance to the tootle nearly as much as they did yesterday.

Noddy hesitates

Tubby Bear Noddy's never played it before.
Big-Ears Maybe that's why.
Noddy (*unable to keep up the lie*) No, Big-Ears. That wasn't the tootle.
Big-Ears What?
Noddy I was playing Tubby's peashooter.
Big-Ears Then where's the tootle?
Tubby Bear I left it on a cloud. (*He points upwards*)
Big-Ears You mean it's... (*He points upwards*)

Tubby Bear nods

   (*With a sudden thought*) But how come (*he indicates the audience*)
   everybody danced?
Noddy I asked them to...
Big-Ears You asked them to play a trick on the Great Tootle?
Noddy Yes. (*Ashamedly*) Sorry, Big-Ears.
Big-Ears I should think so. You should have owned up. Told the Great
   Tootle the truth.
Tubby Bear But Mr Plod would have put me in prison.
Big-Ears Serve you right for taking the tootle in the first place.

Noddy But I thought it would give us time to get the tootle back, Big-Ears.
Big-Ears Get it back? How? It's up there on a cloud!
Noddy If only I could fly, maybe I could fly up to the cloud and get the tootle back. If only I hadn't wasted my wishes.
Tubby Bear (*having an idea*) Big-Ears, couldn't you do some brownie magic?
Big-Ears To make Noddy fly? No, no, Tubby. I haven't done any brownie magic for ages. I'm all rusty.
Noddy Please, Big-Ears. It's our only chance.
Big-Ears Oh, very well. I'll try. (*He takes in the audience*) Everybody concentrate. (*He makes a "fluence" gesture*)

The Lighting sparkles magically. Music for atmosphere. The audience should again join in repeating after Big-Ears during the following

And say after me… (*Chanting*) Abracadabra, Fee Fo Fi
All (including Audience) Abracadabra, Fee Fo Fi
Big-Ears Noddy, I command you fly!
All (including Audience) Noddy, I command you fly!

A big build-up. Noddy flaps his arms and stretches upwards. But he doesn't fly

Big-Ears Sorry, Noddy, I've lost my touch.

Suddenly, exciting Lights and music start as an aeroplane enters. At first, Noddy, Big-Ears and Tubby Bear don't see it, but the audience let them know what has happened. All react amazed and delighted. Exciting music as the scene begins to change and Big-Ears helps Noddy into the cockpit. There is room for two, so Noddy invites Tubby to join him

SCENE 5

Mr Sparks' Garage

Mr Sparks enters

Big-Ears indicates the aeroplane, and Mr Sparks fills it with petrol from his pump. Then Mr Sparks turns the propeller and the engine roars into life. Smoke and sound effect. The propeller whizzes round

(NB: In the original production, it was impractical to return to Mr Sparks' Garage, so Mr Sparks simply entered with the aeroplane, we assumed it was

already full of petrol, and the action continued as described above. Mr Sparks helped Big-Ears assist Noddy and Tubby Bear into the aeroplane)

If the following sequence is done with UV lighting, black curtains will need to fly in as the normal stage Lighting fades down

Big-Ears (*to the audience, encouraging them to join in*) Ten! Nine! Eight! Seven! Six! Five! Four! Three! Two! One! Lift-off!

As the aeroplane lifts off, Big-Ears and Mr Sparks wave farewell and exit

As the aeroplane reaches centre stage, the scene changes to...

SCENE 6

The Sky

A UV sequence, in front of a black background, accompanied by a pre-recorded song

The aeroplane hovers c as puppeteers in black manipulate the objects Noddy and Tubby Bear meet in the sky. For example, clouds, birds, a kite, a hot-air balloon, a space rocket, a flying saucer, and, finally, another cloud—on which is seen the tootle. As the cloud passes by, Noddy manages to retrieve the tootle just before the end of the song

Song 3: Noddy's Aeroplane

Noddy	Oh, if only I could fly.
All	Said Noddy.
Noddy	Like a bird up in the sky
All	Said Noddy.
Noddy	I'd look down
	On Toytown
	Tiny Toytown far away
	I'd wave to
	My friends who
	Would suddenly see me and say
All	Hey!
	Look who's up there in the sky
	It's Noddy

                              Like a bird, who's flying high?
It's Noddy
So happy
So carefree
Gently gliding on the breeze
Yes, guess who
Can soar through
The air with the greatest of ease?

He's
Noddy
Noddy
Noddy in his aeroplane
Noddy
Noddy
Noddy in his aeroplane
Noddy
Noddy
Noddy in his aeroplane
Noddy
Noddy
Noddy in his aeroplane
Up, up, up in the air
Go, go, go anywhere
Noddy
Noddy
Noddy in his aeroplane.

Noddy   Oh, if only I could fly
All   Said Noddy
Noddy   Like a bird up in the sky
All   Said Noddy
His wish has
Come true as
He arrives among the clouds
His dreams are
Up there, far
Away from the maddening crowds

Now
Noddy
Noddy
Noddy in his aeroplane
Noddy

Noddy
Noddy in his aeroplane
Noddy
Noddy
Noddy in his aeroplane
Noddy
Noddy
Noddy in his aeroplane
Up, up, up in the air
Go, go, go anywhere
Noddy
Noddy
Noddy in his aeroplane. (*Repeat and fade as necessary*)

As the music finishes, the aeroplane flies off stage. Noddy and Tubby Bear wave

Black-out

SCENE 7

Toytown Square. The Great Tootle's caravan is in position

As the scene change takes place, Big-Ears enters in an isolated pool of Light

Big-Ears (*to the audience*) Success! The tootle was found! All set for a happy ending! But I didn't know that as I joined the audience for the Great Tootle's performance at six o'clock in the Town Square.

Six bells chime as the Lights come up on the Town Square

The Skittles enter

They approach Big-Ears, who smiles and knocks them over. They giggle with delight and stand up again

The Great Tootle pops out of his caravan

He bangs his drum or his tambourine and, almost magically, draws the Skittles and Big-Ears towards the caravan

Mr Plod and Mr Sparks enter

The Great Tootle uses his drum or tambourine to draw them too towards the caravan

The Great Tootle (*speaking in rhythm and banging his drum*)
>   Roll up! Roll up! Don't be shy!
>   It's your lucky day! Let me tell you why!
>   Roll up! Roll up! Don't be late!
>   Show time! Show time! It's gonna be great!
>   Citizens of Toytown, good day!
>   Gather round! Hear what I say!
>   I'm the Great Tootle and I want you to know
>   It's time to see my magic show!

Applause

>   Watch and wonder! (*He performs an impressive
>   magic trick*)
>   Iggery, jiggery, toot toot toot! Da daaaa!

Applause

And now, my friends, I'd like to introduce you to my tootle. Tootle makes you happy! Tootle makes you smile. Tootle makes you *dance!*

Applause. But Big-Ears looks concerned. The Great Tootle takes out the peashooter from his pocket and starts to blow. Nothing happens. He tries again. Nothing. The audience mutter

Come on tootle, tootle! (*He realizes*) Hey, this isn't my tootle! (*Horrified*) What is it?

A sudden shout turns everyone's heads as Noddy and Tubby Bear enter at speed

Tubby Bear It's my peashooter!
The Great Tootle (*mystified*) Peashooter!
Noddy Sorry, Great Tootle. We gave it to you by mistake.
The Great Tootle But...
Noddy (*proudly*) Here is your tootle. (*He gives it to the Great Tootle and takes the peashooter*)

The Great Tootle, rather confused, plays a tentative toot or two to test the tootle. Every little burst makes everybody start to dance—just a step or two

The Great Tootle (*delighted*) It *is* my tootle! Thank you, Noddy!

All cheer. The Great Tootle shows off his tootle to Mr Plod, Mr Sparks and the Skittles. Noddy gives the peashooter back to Tubby Bear, then goes to Big-Ears

Noddy Thank *you*, Big-Ears.
Big-Ears Me?
Tubby Bear (*joining them*) For your brownie magic.
Big-Ears (*indicating the audience*) Everyone helped!
Noddy
Tubby Bear } (*together*) Thank you!

All cheer

The Great Tootle Come on, everybody! Let's tootle! (*He starts to play*)

All, even Mr Plod, start to dance joyfully. Everybody dances forward, inviting the audience to dance too. The music is still playing and everyone is still dancing as—

—the CURTAIN *falls*

After a short curtain call, it is suggested that the Great Tootle starts tootling again and that everyone, waving goodbye to the audience, dances off

FURNITURE AND PROPERTY LIST

Further dressing may be added at the director's discretion, but should always be faithful to the original illustrations.

NODDY AND THE NOAH'S ARK

Scene 1

Set: Toadstool House, Dark Wood cloth
Post with washing line. *On it*: sheet, pillowcase, pair of trousers, scarf, etc.

Off stage: Basket (**Big-Ears**)

Scene 2

Strike: Toadstool House, Dark Wood cloth

Set: Police Station

Off stage: Collecting tin (**Tessie Bear**)
Rolled-up poster (**Mr Plod**)

Personal: **Sam Skittle:** sixpence
Sally Skittle: sixpence
Mr Plod: sixpence, whistle

Scene 3

Strike: Police Station

Set: **Noddy**'s House

Off stage: Collecting tin (**Tessie Bear**)
Washing basket (**Noddy**)
Washing basket (**Sly**)
Bicycle (**Big-Ears**)

Personal: **Noddy:** sixpence
                Tessie Bear: biscuit

SCENE 4

Strike: **Noddy**'s House

Set: Police Station
                Folded note pinned to door, saying "READ ME"

SCENE 5

Strike: Police Station

Set: **Mr Noah**'s Ark and gangplank

SCENE 6

Strike: **Mr Noah**'s Ark

Set: Dark Wood cloth
                Washing basket containing washing, poster, collecting tin

Off stage: Torch (**Mr Plod**)

Personal: **Bumpy Dog: Big Ears'** white sheet and white pillowcase

SCENE 7

Strike: Dark Wood cloth

Set: **Mr Noah**'s Ark

Personal: **Mr Plod:** collecting tin

NODDY AND THE TOOTLE

SCENE 1

Strike: **Mr Noah**'s Ark

Set: **Mr Sparks'** Garage
                Petrol pump

Off stage: Bicycle (**Big-Ears**)
Car. *On passenger seat*: bucket and sponge
Satchel containing bottle with lemonade (**Tubby Bear**)
Picnic rug, basket containing jam tarts (**SM**)

SCENE 2

Personal: **Tubby Bear:** peashooter

SCENE 3

Set: Toytown Square

Off stage: Small caravan containing drum or tambourine (**The Great Tootle**)

Personal: **Mr Plod:** whistle, notebook
The Great Tootle: piece of paper, three-coloured magic wand, tootle

SCENE 4

Strike: Toytown Square

Set: **Noddy**'s House

Off stage: Aeroplane, puppet **Tubby Bear** (**SM**)

Personal: **Noddy:** wishing wand
Tubby Bear: peashooter
Noddy: peashooter

SCENE 5

Strike: **Noddy**'s House

Set: **Mr Sparks**' Garage

SCENE 6

Strike: **Mr Sparks**' Garage

Set: UV sequence black background

Off stage: Clouds, birds, kite, hot-air balloon, space rocket, flying saucer, cloud with tootle (**SM**)

SCENE 7

Strike: UV sequence black background

Set: Toytown Square
              Caravan

Off stage: Tambourine (**The Great Tootle**)
              Tootle (**Noddy**)

Personal: **The Great Tootle:** peashooter

LIGHTING PLOT

Property fittings required: nil
Practical fittings: police lamp
Various interior and exterior locations

ACT I, SCENE 1

To open: Overall general lighting

No cues

ACT I, SCENE 2

To open: Overall general lighting. Snap on police lamp

Cue 1   **Sly** exits   (Page 9)
               Black-out, then fade up lighting on **Big-Ears** *and*
               Whiskers

ACT I, SCENE 3

Cue 2   A loud "parp-parp" from off stage   (Page 10)
               Fade up lights on **Noddy**'*s house*

ACT I, SCENE 4

To open: Overall general lighting

No cues

ACT I, SCENE 5

To open: Overall general lighting

Cue 3   **All**: "Oh yeah!"   (Page 19)
             Fade to black-out

ACT I, Scene 6

To open: Shady, mysterious lighting. When ready bring up torch beam effect to
             cover Plod's torch

Cue 4   **Plod**: "Aaaah!"   (Page 20)
             Cut torch-covering spot

ACT I, Scene 7

Cue 5   A big fanfare sounds   (Page 25)
             Lights up on **Mr Noah**'s *Ark*

ACT II, Scene 1

To open: Overall general lighting

Cue 6   Car makes "parp-parp" sound   (Page 32)
             Change lighting

ACT II, Scene 2

To open: Bright sunny day lighting

*No cue*s

ACT II, Scene 3

To open: Overall general lighting

Cue 7   **The Great Tootle** returns to his caravan   (Page 41)
             Fade to moonlight

Cue 8   **Tubby Bear** exits   (Page 41)
             Fade to black-out

ACT II, Scene 4

Cue 9	**Noddy** emerges from his house *Bring up lighting*	(Page 41)
Cue 10	**Noddy**: "...a really good wish..." *Dramatic lighting*	(Page 42)
Cue 11	**Noddy**: "...and don't come back!" *Magical lighting*	(Page 43)
Cue 12	**Noddy**: "I wish I had Big-Ears...!" *Dramatic lighting*	(Page 44)
Cue 13	**Noddy** concentrates in his wishing position *Atmospheric lighting*	(Page 46)
Cue 14	**Noddy** goes behind the house *Change lighting*	(Page 46)
Cue 15	**Big-Ears** strikes a magical pose *Magical lighting*	(Page 47)
Cue 16	**Noddy**: "Wish I Tubby!" *Change lighting; continue*	(Page 47)
Cue 17	**Tubby Bear** enters in reverse *End lighting changes*	(Page 48)
Cue 18	**Big-Ears** makes a "fluence" gesture *Bring up magically sparkling lighting*	(Page 51)
Cue 19	**Big-Ears**: "Sorry, Noddy, I've lost my touch." *Bring up exciting lighting*	(Page 51)

ACT II, Scene 5

To open: Exciting lighting

Cue 20	When ready *Fade down lighting*	(Page 52)

ACT II, SCENE 6

To open: UV lighting

Cue 21   **Noddy** and **Tubby Bear** fly off stage   (Page 54)
              Black-out

ACT II, SCENE 7

Cue 22   **Big-Ears** enters   (Page 54)
              Pool of light on Big-Ears

Cue 23   **Big-Ears**: "...six o'clock in the Town Square."   (Page 54)
              Bring up lighting on Town Square

EFFECTS PLOT

ACT I

Cue 1	**Big-Ears**: "It's been a perfect drying morning!" **Whiskers'** *miaows as script pages 1 - 2*	(Page 1)
Cue 2	**Big-Ears**: "One day…" *Car "parp-parp, parp-parp!" sound off stage*	(Page 2)
Cue 3	**Noddy**: "Morning, Whiskers." **Whiskers** *miaows*	(Page 3)
Cue 4	**Noddy** presses the car horn *Car "parp-parp" sound*	(Page 5)
Cue 5	**Whiskers** pops up from behind the house **Whiskers** *miaows nervously*	(Page 5)
Cue 6	To open Scene 3 *Loud car "parp-parp" sound off stage*	(Page 10)
Cue 7	To open Scene 5 *Car "parp-parp, parp-parp" sound off stage*	(Page 15)
Cue 8	**Noddy**: "Mr Noah?" *Cacophony of animal noises*	(Page 15)
Cue 9	**Mr Noah**: "Calm, shipmates, calm." *Animal noises subside*	(Page 15)
Cue 10	**Mr Noah**: "Will we, shipmates?" *Cacophony of animal noises*	(Page 16)
Cue 11	**Mr Noah**: "Calm, shipmates, calm!" *Animal noises fade*	(Page 16)
Cue 12	**Mr Noah** is stunned into silence *Sad, groaning animal cacophony*	(Page 16)

| *Cue* 13 | To open Scene 6 | (Page 19) |
| | *Spooky sound effects* | |

| *Cue* 14 | **Mr Plod**: "Sly!" | (Page 19) |
| | *Owl hoot* | |

| *Cue* 15 | **Mr Plod**: "What's that?" | (Page 20) |
| | *Owl hoot* | |

| *Cue* 16 | **Mr Plod**: "…bold and brave and fearless." | (Page 20) |
| | *Owl hoot* | |

ACT II

| *Cue* 17 | **Noddy** enters from garage | (Page 31) |
| | *Clanking and banging in garage* | |

| *Cue* 18 | **Mr Sparks**: "Afternoon, Noddy!" | (Page 31) |
| | *Cut clanking and banging, car "parp-parp" sound off stage* | |

| *Cue* 19 | **Noddy**: "Feeling better?" | (Page 32) |
| | *Car "parp-parp" sound* | |

| *Cue* 20 | **Big-Ears**: "…we need to go back to last week…" | (Page 32) |
| | *Tape rewinding effect* | |

| *Cue* 21 | **Noddy** takes bucket and sponge from car | (Page 32) |
| | *Cut tape rewinding effect* | |

| *Cue* 22 | **Tubby Bear** pours lemonade into car petrol tank | (Page 33) |
| | *"Glug glug" sound* | |

| *Cue* 23 | **Noddy** turns on the engine | (Page 33) |
| | *Sound effect of an auto-hiccup, repeated as appropriate* | |

| *Cue* 24 | **Big-Ears**: "Now back to today…" | (Page 33) |
| | *Tape fast forward effect, cut when ready* | |

| *Cue* 25 | As music ends at start of Scene 2 | (Page 35) |
| | *Birdsong* | |

| *Cue* 26 | **Big-Ears**: "What a perfect afternoon." | (Page 35) |
| | *Angry buzzing of a wasp* | |

Cue 27   **Noddy**: "I'd rather not take the risk."   (Page 35)
            Cut wasp buzzing, start again, and cut

Cue 28   **Big-Ears**: "I've been stung!"   (Page 35)
            Wasp buzzing

Cue 29   **Big-Ears** rubs his bottom   (Page 35)
            Fade buzzing

Cue 30   **Noddy**: "...think of a really good wish..."   (Page 42)
            Flash and dramatic sound effects

Cue 31   **Noddy**: "...and don't come back!"   (Page 43)
            Flash and magical sound effects

Cue 32   **Tubby Bear** takes off   (Page 44)
            Exciting take-off noises

Cue 33   Puppet **Tubby Bear** flies away   (Page 44)
            Fade sound effects

Cue 34   **Noddy**: "I wish I had Big-Ears...!"   (Page 44)
            Flash and dramatic sound effects, smoke

Cue 35   **Noddy** retreats behind his house   (Page 44)
            Fade effects

Cue 36   **Noddy** goes behind the house   (Page 46)
            Flash, sound effects and smoke

Cue 37   **Noddy**: "Wish I Tubby!"   (Page 47)
            Dramatic sound effects (optional)

Cue 38   **Tubby Bear** enters in reverse   (Page 48)
            Buzzing noise, then cut

Cue 39   **Mr Sparks** turns the propeller   (Page 51)
            Smoke and engine noise

Cue 40   To open Scene 6   (Page 52)
            Pre-recorded music

Cue 41   **Big-Ears**: "...at six o'clock in the Town Square." (Page 54)
            Six bells chime